Key Definitions for Economics A Level Revision

3rd Edition

For OCR Students

Mark Jewell

anforme limited

© Anforme Ltd 2008

ISBN 978-1-905504-22-0

Anforme Limited
Stocksfield Hall, Stocksfield
Northumberland NE43 7TN

Typeset by George Wishart & Associates, Whitley Bay.
Printed by Potts, Cramlington.

Contents

Markets in Action

Basic Concepts

1	**Scarcity**	Where wants for a product (or factor of production) exceed amount available (where demand exceeds supply at zero price)
		Additional information: Supposedly inevitable consequence of man's innate desire to have more (unlimited wants); leads to need for a rationing system like prices (very scarce goods have higher prices). Goods can be classified either economic goods (i.e. scarce) or free goods (not scarce, e.g. air)
2	**Factor of Production**	A productive resource
		Additional information: 4 types: land (all natural resources e.g. forests, fish, oil, soils and land area), labour (by quantity and quality, skills etc), capital and enterprise
3	**Capital**	Man-made aids to production
		Additional information: e.g. machine (iMac) or building; often confused with 'financial capital', which relates to a sum of money
4	**Enterprise (Entrepreneurship)**	The risk-taking role undertaken by owners of a business as they combine other factors of production in the pursuit of profit
		Additional information: A key factor of production in a market economy (a specialised form of labour)
5	**Investment (Unit 1)** (I)	Spending by firms on new capital stock or repair of existing stock (per period)
		Additional information: Not to be confused with saving, which is what people do when they buy stocks and shares (think of this as financial investment); net I = gross I − depreciation (= addition to firms' capital stock per period: enabling PPF to shift out); N.B. gross I = total firms' I spending (this is the item in the Aggregate Demand equation)
6	**Depreciation** (of capital)	The rate at which capital loses value over time
		Additional information: Occurs due to wear and tear or through technological obsolescence; means gross investment must exceed depreciation for the capital stock to increase (to shift PPF out next year)

7	**Opportunity Cost** (O/C)	The value (benefit) of the next best preferred option foregone

Additional information:
e.g. i. opportunity cost of having a child could be the holidays one would have been able to go on instead, ii. opportunity cost of increased UK consumption this year is increased consumption next year (from boosting investment today)

8	**Production Possibility Curve** (PPC)	The combinations of two goods which an economy is capable of producing using all its resources in the most efficient way

Additional information:
Also known as production possibility frontier (PPF) shows opportunity cost: moving from inside to on PPC carries no opportunity cost; moving around PPC involves giving up 1 good for the other; PPC is curved out from origin

9	**Allocative Efficiency** (Unit 1)	Where resources are used to produce what consumers actually want to buy i.e. where resources are allocated such that no consumer could be made better off without another consumer becoming worse off (Pareto optimality)

Additional information:
Not only is production on the PPC but the combination of goods matches consumer wants; see 106 for more technical detail

10	**Pareto Efficiency**	Where resources are allocated such that it is impossible to make someone better off without making someone else worse off

Additional information:
All points inside a society's production possibility frontier cannot be Pareto efficient since more of at least one of the goods can be produced with no reduction in the output of others; Pareto efficiency demands both maximum productive and allocative efficiency; however, whilst a great many potential outcomes may be Pareto optimal, many of these will be highly inequitable

11	**Specialisation**	Where a factor of production is devoted to a specific job in the production process

Additional information:
e.g. labour can specialise (your Economics teacher probably doesn't sing professionally or teach French), land usually has a specialist use (Bordeaux vineyards are not used for car manufacture or even pea growing); if resources specialise in what they have a comparative advantage in, this enables larger scale production and there are significant efficiency gains (enabling an economy to move towards its production possibility curve): mass production methods for car manufacture become possible etc.

12	**Division of Labour**	Where labour specialises in the performance of a particular part of the production process
		Additional information: This is a form of specialisation (an economy of scale); made famous in Adam Smith's 'Wealth of Nations' (1776) with his example of pinmaking and its different stages of production

13	**Money**	Whatever is generally acceptable in exchange for goods and services or labour
		Additional information: The most obvious forms of money in developed economies are cash and bank deposits (when paying by cheque), although credit card company credit is accepted by most retailers as payment for goods; money must fulfil 4 functions: i. medium of exchange, ii. unit of account, iii. store of value, iv. standard for deferred payments; to succeed, money must have several key characteristics being: divisible, durable, portable, recognisable, controllable in supply and not intrinsically valuable

14	**Unit Cost (Average Cost)** (AC)	Cost per unit of output
		Additional information: AC = total cost/output; falls when firm expands in long run and benefits from economies of scale (see 120); rises if firm has to increase output in the short run due to diminishing marginal returns (see 112); productive efficiency is only maximised when AC is at its minimum (see 105)

15	**Positive Economics**	The study of propositions which can be verified (proved or disproved) by data from the real world
		Additional information: e.g. "inflation is 2% in UK"

16	**Normative Economics**	The study of propositions which cannot be verified by data from the real world and require value judgments
		Additional information: e.g. "inflation should be reduced"

	Section B:	**Basic Operation of Product Markets**

17	**Demand** (D)	The quantity of a good consumers are willing and able to buy at a given price per period
		Additional information: Shift factors: income, tastes, price of complements and substitutes, expected price, population; the 'law of demand' says demand is inversely related to price, ceteris paribus e.g when price falls demand rises (seen as a slide down a given demand curve)

18	**Supply** (S)	The quantity of a good producers are willing and able to sell at a given price per period

Additional information:
Shift factors: cost of production, sales tax or subsidy, expected price, weather, profitability of producer substitutes, technological advance; supply is positively related to price, ceteris paribus e.g. at higher prices more will be willingly supplied by producers (who need higher unit revenue to offset the rise in unit cost associated with the diminishing marginal returns from expanding production in the short run): seen as a slide up the supply curve

19	**Market**	Institution where buyers are in contact with sellers to arrange sale of products

Additional information:
Not to be confused with the building!

20	**Equilibrium**	The price and quantity (traded) which is acceptable to both buyers and sellers so long as conditions of demand and supply stay constant i.e. neither excess demand or excess supply exists at this market price, with these D and S curves

Additional information:
Also known as market equilibrium

21	**Ceteris Paribus**	All other factors remaining constant

Additional information:
Assumption made when drawing single demand or supply curves; breaking it causes shifts in the curves

22	**Disequilibrium**	A combination of price and quantity traded which has a tendency to change for the given demand and supply conditions (curves)

Additional information:
This will be either where excess demand exists at the price (pulling price up – as sellers realise they can still sell all their goods and/or buyers outbid each other, afraid of missing out) or excess supply (price goes down – as sellers cut price to get rid of unsold stock)

23	**Joint Demand**	When demand for one good involves demand for another good (complement)

Additional information:
e.g. DVD player and DVDs; bacon and eggs (rise in price of bacon will lead to leftward shift in demand for eggs)

24	**Joint Supply**	Where supply of one good necessarily involves supply of another

Additional information:
e.g. beef and leather; beeswax and honey (rise in demand for beeswax will shift demand out raising wax price via a slide up the supply curve; this then raises supply of honey too, pushing down honey price via a rightward shift in supply curve for honey)

25	**Consumer Surplus** (CS)	Measure of consumer welfare: the maximum price a consumer is willing to pay for a good minus the market price
		Additional information: Shown by (triangular) area between demand curve and market price

26	**Producer Surplus** (PS)	Measure of producer welfare: the surplus of market price received over the minimum price the producer would be prepared to accept
		Additional information: Shown by (triangular) area between supply curve and market price

27	**Elasticity of Demand** (PeD)	The responsiveness of quantity demanded to a change in price (ceteris paribus)
		Additional information: PeD = % change in Qd/% change in P; if PeD is greater than 1 (ignoring negative sign): relatively elastic, if PeD is less than 1 (ignoring negative sign): relatively inelastic, PeD = (-) 1: unitary elasticity; determinants: no. of close substitutes, luxury or necessity, brand loyalty, habit/time period, % income, durable good

28	**Income Elasticity of Demand** (YeD)	The responsiveness of quantity demanded to a change in income (ceteris paribus)
		Additional information: YeD = % change in Qd/% change in income; positive value = normal good (luxury = high); negative value = inferior good

29	**Cross Elasticity of Demand** (XeD)	The responsiveness of quantity demanded of one good (A) to a change in price of another (B) (ceteris paribus)
		Additional information: XeD = % change Qd (A)/% change P (B); negative value = complementary goods; positive value = substitute goods; zero = unrelated goods

30	**Elasticity of Supply** (PeS)	The responsiveness of quantity supplied to a change in price (ceteris paribus)
		Additional information: PeS = % change in Qs/% change in P; determinants: time period, complexity of production process, availability of factors of production, stocks

31	**Normal Good**	Good whose demand rises as income rises
		Additional information: Includes luxuries and necessities; is opposite of inferior good

32	**Inferior Good**	Good whose demand falls as income rises
		Additional information: Opposite of normal good e.g. supermarket 'economy' toilet paper
33	**Substitute Good**	Good which is an alternative to a particular good from the consumer's point of view
		Additional information: e.g. UK bacon and Danish bacon; if substitute goes up in price, the other good's D curve shifts right
34	**Sales Tax** (Indirect Tax)	Tax levied on the sale of goods
		Additional information: Can be specific (unit) or ad valorem (%); raises firms costs therefore shifts S curve up; may be used by government to deter consumption of demerit goods (e.g. cigarettes) or goods with external costs (e.g. petrol)
35	**Subsidy**	Government payment to producer for production of goods intended to lower the market price
		Additional information: Reduces firm's costs therefore shifts S curve vertically down; may be used by government to encourage greater consumption of merit goods (e.g. dental care) or goods with external benefit (e.g. education)
	Section C:	**Economic Systems**
36	**Economic System**	The institutional means for resolving the problems of resource allocation in an economy (i.e. *what* to produce, *how* to produce it and *to whom* should it go)
		Additional information: 3 types: free market (capitalist) economy, mixed economy, command (planned) economy
37	**Mixed Economy**	Where resource allocation is undertaken by state planning *and* market forces, depending on the product
		Additional information: State planning addresses the problems of market failure, otherwise markets are allowed to function with minimal intervention
38	**Capitalist (Free Market) Economy**	Where markets determine resource allocation with minimal state intervention
		Additional information: State usually protects private property by providing a judicial system

39	**'Invisible Hand'**	Where resources are allocated by the decentralised decision making of consumers and producers acting through markets, without any centralised (state) planning

Additional information:
Advantage of free market system (no bureaucrats needed)

40	**Consumer Sovereignty**	The production of goods is directed by consumer demand

Additional information:
Key advantage of free market system since resources are not wasted on what is not wanted (promoting allocative efficiency) and firms compete by cutting costs (leading to productive efficiency)

	Section D:	**Market Failure Concepts**

41	**Market Failure**	Where free market outcomes lead to major problems for society, usually inefficiency

Additional information:
5 main types (monopoly, public goods, (de)merit goods, externalities, asymmetric information) + inequality

42	**Public Good**	A good with non-excludability and non-rivalry (which is therefore almost impossible for private firms to sell profitably)

Additional Information:
Non-excludability = where once provided the good is available to all at zero cost (i.e. it is impossible to charge for use); non-rivalry = where one person's consumption does not reduce the amount available to other consumers e.g. national defence, street lighting (local); N.B. quasi public goods are those which almost have these features e.g. roads could exclude by tolls (but usually don't – impractical?) and get 'rivalrous' when congested

43	**Merit Good**	A good which consumers underconsume at market prices because they underestimate the long term benefits to themselves

Additional information:
e.g. dental treatment, inoculations against disease (fear of the jab!) and education

44	**Demerit Good**	A good which consumers overconsume at market prices because they underestimate the long term harm to themselves

Additional information:
e.g. hard drugs, gambling. Note: damaging effects hit the consumer himself (e.g. lung cancer from smoking)

45	**Asymmetric Information**	Situation where buyers know more about the value of a product than sellers (or vice versa)
		Additional information: Source of market failure: health insurance markets tend to collapse since buyers know more about their potential claims; professional services (e.g. doctors, lawyers) may need regulation since sellers are better informed about the quality of their advice
46	**Negative Externality**	A side effect of a market activity which harms third parties without compensation
		Additional information: Note: damaging effects harm others (e.g. passive smoking)
47	**Positive Externality**	A side effect of a market activity which benefits third parties without them having to pay
		Additional information: e.g. education, inoculation, nice front garden
48	**Optimal Tax**	Tax equal to marginal external cost (persuading profit maximising firms to choose socially optimal production)
		Additional information: Ideal solution for negative externalities (internalising the external cost) but requires accurate information and enforcement
49	**Regulation**	Rules from government requiring firms to modify their production techniques, output or price
		Additional information: Crude solution to externality problem requiring government to measure the externalities and set suitable limits which are enforceable
50	**Tradable Permit**	A legal right to pollute a fixed amount which can be bought or sold between firms
		Additional information: Government establishes where the socially optimal production is and divides up the level of pollution existing here into tradable units
51	**Government Failure**	Where government intervention causes inefficiency in resource allocation
		Additional information: Several sources: i. inadequate information (e.g. not knowing marginal external costs and setting inoptimal tax), ii. distorting the market by price controls (e.g. high minimum prices for EU farmers leads to overproduction of food and keeps land and farmers in low productive uses), iii. administrative costs etc.

Unit 2:
Section A:

The National and International Economy
Basic Concepts

52	**Macro Economics**	Study of behaviour of an economy as a whole

Additional information:
Concerning e.g. what determines inflation in UK?

53	**Micro Economics**	Study of behaviour of parts of the economy

Additional information:
Concerning individual markets, firms or industries e.g. what determines the price of TVs in UK?

Section B:
Measuring National Economic Performance

54	**Unemployment** (U/E)	The number of people of working age who are seeking work yet do not have a paid job

Additional Information:
Unemployment rate is = numbers unemployed/workforce ...where workforce = unemployed + employed = economically active = all those either in work or looking for work

55	**Economic Activity Rate**	Those either looking for work or in work as a proportion of the population of working age

Additional information:
Also known as participation rate; increased activity rate will promote growth of GDP

56	**Economically Inactive**	Those of working age who have chosen not to do paid work or look for paid work

Additional information:
Includes: houseworkers, students (over school leaving age, currently 16), early retired

57	**Gross Domestic Product** (GDP)	The value of output produced by domestic based resources per year

Additional information:
Understates true output since DIY etc not counted but overstates it if net external costs are generated; per capita GDP is a simple measure of average living standards; differs from GNP (gross national product) only because GDP excludes the net income flow arising from foreign ownership of assets (i.e. interest, dividends and profits)

58	**Economic Growth**	Rate of increase in national output per year

Additional information:
National output = gross domestic product i.e. the value of output produced by domestic based resources p.a.; this term is usually associated with real growth

59	**Real Growth**	Growth of GDP after inflation has been accounted for (i.e. at constant prices)

Additional information:
This is the key measure of national economic performance; is on the horizontal axis of AD/AS graphs and is therefore stimulated by an increase (shift right) in either AD or AS

60	**Nominal Growth**	Growth of GDP before inflation has been accounted for (i.e. at current prices)

Additional information:
Nominal growth rate – inflation rate = real growth rate (approximately)

61	**Sustainable Development**	Development which meets the needs of present generations without reducing the ability of future generations to meet their needs

Additional information:
This means bequesting at least the same value of wealth to future generations from which they can derive at least identical income (i.e. any deterioration in finite land resources must be compensated by enhanced physical and human capital)

62	**Inflation** ($\dot{P}$)	The rate of change in the average price level

Additional information:
RPI measures level of retail prices at a point in time; inflation (year 1-2) = RPI (year 2) – RPI (year 1)/RPI (year 1) x 100; RPI includes all retail prices (weighted in proportion to household spending); RPIX excludes mortgage interest repayments (therefore if interest rates increase, RPI rises but RPIX doesn't); Consumer Price Index (CPI) (see 64 for definition)

63	**Retail Price Index** (RPI)	Weighted average of the retail price level at a point in time (expressed as an index number)

Additional information:
Weights reflect % household spending; arguably overstates the cost of living since the weights are slow to change and quality of goods generally increases (so value rises despite increase in price)

64	**Consumer Price Index** (CPI)	An index number measuring a weighted average for the price of consumer goods and services at a point in time

Additional information:
Superceded RPIX as a target for inflation by the Bank of England after 2003 as more internationally comparable and broader (includes financial services, but excludes council tax)

65	**Underlying Inflation** (RPIX)	RPI excluding mortgage interest payments

Additional information:
The Bank of England targeted RPIX at 2.5% between 1997-2003, when considering interest rate change. After 2003 it targeted the related measure of the Consumer Prices Index (CPI) at 2.0%; RPIY also measures underlying inflation (= RPIX – indirect tax)

66	**Balance of Payments** (BoP)	A record of the transactions between residents of one country and those living abroad over a year

Additional information:
Split into current and financial (formerly 'capital') accounts; these sum to zero i.e. balance overall

67	**Balance of Payments Current Account**	The net inflow of money to a country arising from international trade in goods and services, investment income and transfers

Additional information:
A deficit means more money leaving a country (e.g. from import spending) than entering it (e.g. from export earnings); vice versa for a surplus

68	**Investment Income**	Earnings from ownership of assets

Additional information:
Includes: **I**nterest from savings deposits or lending/borrowing, **P**rofits from companies and **D**ividends from shares ('I.P.D.'); is measured in the Balance of Payments current account, where inflows of such earnings from owning assets abroad count as [+] credit items (offset by outflows abroad: [–] debits)

	Section C:	**Circular Flow of Income**

69	**Circular Flow of Income**	Model which explains what determines the equilibrium level of national income

Additional information:
Model shows spending and income flows between domestic households and firms; equilibrium is reached when: national output = national income = national expenditure (= aggregate demand) and where injections = withdrawals (see 70-71)

70	**Injection** (J)	Spending on domestic output which comes from outside the simple circular flow of income i.e. investment, government and exports

Additional information:
This has a magnified effect on final national income by the action of the Multiplier (see 72)

71	**Withdrawal** (W)	Income which is not spent on domestic output (consumption) i.e. savings, taxation and imports
		Additional information: Tends to reduce the strength of the Multiplier (see 72)
72	**Multiplier Effect**	The knock-on effects of an initial change in injections or withdrawals which cause national income to change by more than the initial change
		Additional information: A downward (negative) Multiplier effect means an initial reduction in income will become worse after households have reduced their spending causing firms to pay out even less income; vice versa for an upward Multiplier effect; Multiplier = change in GDP/change in J (or W); size of Multiplier is boosted by high marginal propensity to consume (= that proportion of an increase in income which consumers spend on domestic output)
	Section D:	**Theory of Aggregate Demand and Supply**
73	**Aggregate Demand** (AD)	The sum of all planned spending on domestic output at a given general price level per period
		Additional information: AD = C + I + G + X – M (for C and I: see 75, 76) G is government spending on public services (i.e. excludes any transfer payments made to anyone who did no productive work to earn e.g. pensions, but includes wages to NHS staff etc.) X is spending by foreigners on UK exports; M is spending by UK residents on imports (subtracted since C etc. includes some imports); 'demand pull inflation' is caused when rightward shifts in AD causes slide up the AS curve
74	**Aggregate Supply** (AS)	The sum of all planned domestic production at a given general price level per period
		Additional information: AS increases as firms become more able and willing to produce extra output; policies designed to shift AS right are 'supply side policies' (see 92); where AS curve shifts left through rising costs (e.g. rise in nominal wage inflation, price of oil, etc.) this creates 'cost push inflation'
75	**Consumption** (C)	Spending by domestic households on consumer goods and services
		Additional information: Is determined by: current income, wealth, interest rate, expected income, tax rates, inflation, demography etc.

76	**Investment (Unit 2)** (I)	Spending by domestic firms on capital goods
		Additional information: Investment spending yields returns into the future hence includes new buildings and (in theory) training of staff; is determined by interest rate, change in demand (accelerator) and business confidence (expected revenues); also includes house building
77	**Wealth Effect**	A rise in personal wealth will encourage consumers to spend more and save less
		Additional information: Rises in wealth come from: e.g. rise in house values, rise in stock market
78	**Recession**	Declining real GDP for two successive quarters (six months)
		Additional information: Occurs during the slowdown ('bust') in economic activity as part of the economic cycle, associated with falling AD; solutions: government could boost AD by cutting interest rates, taxes etc (Keynesian approach) or enable prices and wages to fall more effectively thereby boosting AS (Classical approach)
79	**Demand Management**	Where government attempts to control aggregate demand by adjusting tax rates, interest rates and government spending in order to avoid 'booms' (high inflation) and 'busts' (high unemployment)
		Additional information: Also known as 'fine tuning'; but now discredited due to problems of time lags etc., as supply side policies have come to be seen as more effective in delivering long term non-inflationary growth
80	**Fiscal Policy**	Manipulation of government spending and taxation to achieve macro economic goals
		Additional information: No longer used to 'fine tune' AD in the economy, although automatic stabilisers (see 325) will ensure budget deficit helps to modify the effects of recession on unemployment etc
81	**Direct Tax**	Tax levied on an individual or company on their income or wealth
		Additional information: e.g. UK income tax, corporation tax, council tax, capital gains tax; usually progressive but unlike indirect taxes can reduce incentives to work (see 158)
82	**Indirect Tax**	Tax levied on expenditure
		Additional information: e.g. in UK: VAT, tobacco duty, fuel duty

83	**Monetary Policy**	Manipulation of interest rates to achieve macro economic goals

Additional information:
Since 1997 Bank of England's Monetary Policy Committee has set interest rate to target inflation (2.0% CPI since 2003), so UK government not in direct control; in theory, after 2 year lag, a rise in interest rate will reduce inflation via a fall in AD (higher mortgage repayments reduces C, higher cost of borrowing reduces I etc.)

84	**Exchange Rate** (ER)	The price of one currency in terms of another (e.g. £1 = $2)

Additional information:
Determined in currency market by interaction of demand for, say, £'s by foreign buyers of UK exports (etc) and supply of £'s by UK importers of foreign goods (etc). D for £'s depends on foreign income, competitiveness of UK exports (i.e. UK domestic inflation), tastes, expected Sterling exchange rate, UK relative interest rate; fall in exchange rate encourages exports and fall in imports (and Balance of Payments current balance should rise)

85	**Competitiveness**	The ability of domestic firms to sell their output in the global market (domestic + foreign)

Additional information:
Firms need to stay competitive to survive and contribute to GDP and preserve jobs; this implies being competitive on price or non-price (product quality, branding etc): former helped by fall in exchange rate, non-inflationary wage settlements, higher productivity (e.g. lower unit labour costs); latter by supply side policies (e.g. higher skills)

86	**Foreign Currency Market**	The institutional arrangements whereby people can buy and sell foreign currency at an agreed exchange rate

Additional information:
e.g. buyers of pounds sterling (foreign importers of UK exports, foreign tourists to UK etc) sell foreign currency for £ via foreign exchange dealers to those in UK wanting it (e.g. for importing foreign goods, visiting abroad on holiday etc)

87	**Interest Rate** (r)	The price of liquidity (money in a spendable form e.g. bank deposits or cash)

Additional information:
i.e. what has to be paid in the future for a loan now; cuts in r encourage more spending due to reduced mortgage repayments, cheaper credit and more investment; real r = nominal r minus inflation (= the price of borrowed funds in terms of purchasing power); in times of very high inflation, high nominal r can mean negative real r i.e. borrowing is cheap (loan can be repaid out of inflated nominal income); with deflation (i.e. falling general price level), government cannot set nominal r below zero yet real r is increased by falls in the general price level (making monetary policy ineffective)

88	**Disposable Income** (Yd)	Household income after subtracting direct taxes (income tax and national insurance contributions) and adding government benefit payments

Additional information:
Consumption spending (C) in AD is boosted if Yd rises; hence government can stimulate AD by tax cuts when gross incomes have not risen

89	**Flexible Labour Market**	A competitive (macro) labour market in which employers and workers are free to negotiate market wages and conditions of work, in which workers are adaptable to the labour needs of firms and firms are adaptable to workers' needs

Additional information:
This involves: 1. no distortions to the labour markets e.g. national minimum wages, trade unions, monopsony employer, 2. labour which is occupationally and geographically mobile (e.g. capable of retraining), 3. employers who can offer part-time work etc to enable workers (usually female) to balance child care with paid work

90	**Classical Unemployment**	Unemployment due to real wages being held above market-clearing level

Additional information:
Sometimes called 'real wage unemployment'; caused by excessive national minimum wage or trade union pressure; solutions: abolish national minimum wage or weaken trade union power!

91	**Demand Deficient (Cyclical) Unemployment**	Unemployment caused by the fall in demand for labour which accompanies a fall in aggregate demand (and where real wages don't fall: wages are 'sticky downwards')

Additional information:
Sometimes called 'cyclical unemployment' or 'Keynesian unemployment'; wages may be sticky because of trade unions but accepting a real wage cut across the macro economy may not solve the problem since AD would fall further; solution: government reflation (G rise or cut in tax or interest rates)

92	**Supply Side Policies**	Government attempts to increase aggregate supply

Additional information:
e.g. cutting tax rates to improve incentives to work, encouraging greater participation rate in the labour market, reducing monopoly power, privatisation, boosting education and training; all such policies shift AS curve to the right, which tends to reduce inflation and increase employment and real growth

93	**Frictional Unemployment**	Workers moving between jobs who are unable to fill job vacancies between contracts due to imperfect information in the labour market

Additional information:
Sometimes called 'search unemployment'; unemployed (supply of labour) coexist with job vacancies (demand for labour); solution: improve job centres, cut unemployment benefit levels to speed up job search! (though some frictional unemployment is healthy: enables workless to find the most suitable job for their skill levels)

94	**Structural Occupational Unemployment**	Unemployment due to mismatch of skills demanded (in job vacancies) and skills supplied by the unemployed within a region

Additional information:
Cause is the change in structure of industry forced by changing demand or cost conditions e.g. unemployed miners in S Wales can't fill nearby job vacancies in IT; solution is not to increase AD (enough vacancies exist for all unemployed), but to help unemployed retrain in the new sectors

95	**Structural Geographical Unemployment**	Unemployment due to geographical mismatch between the job vacancies and the unemployed with those skills

Additional information:
In UK, unemployed may be unable or reluctant to travel to different parts of the country for work due to local social ties or the large house price gradient to the south east; the solution is not retraining or raising AD, but to use regional aid or dismantle Green Belt building restrictions in the south east

96	**Seasonal Unemployment**	Unemployment due to downturn in demand for certain types of labour at certain times of year

Additional information:
e.g. builders in winter, waiters in off peak tourist season, farm labourers in non-harvest time

97	**Technological Unemployment**	Unemployment due to the substitution of labour by capital when technology advances

Additional information:
Highly visible cause of temporary unemployment but labour is capable of retraining or moving to other jobs; rapid technological advance hasn't prevented UK unemployment from falling in 1990s or stopping agricultural workers getting industrial jobs when industrial revolution occurred; solution: encourage retraining (market provides the incentive for this already)

98	**EU Enlargement**	Process whereby the established 15 members of the European Union is widening its membership to new European (accession) countries

Additional information:
In May 2004, 10 new countries joined (Poland, Hungary, Czech Republic, Slovakia, Slovenia, Estonia, Latvia, Lithuania, Republic of Cyprus, Malta); in January 2007, Bulgaria and Romania joined; candidates for future enlargement include Croatia and, controversially, Turkey; EU membership requires a country to fulfil conditions of political and economic development before entry

Section E:	**Trade Policy**

99	**Free Trade**	International trade in goods and services without trade barriers

Additional information:
Enables producers to specialise in areas where they have a comparative advantage to mutual trading gain; World Trade Organisation promotes the removal of trade barriers e.g. tariffs and quotas

100	**Protectionism**	The raising of trade barriers against imports

Additional information:
This protects domestic industry from more competitive foreign firms by the raising of tariffs, quotas or bureaucratic barriers; it is rational to respond to protectionist measures in kind, but it causes deadweight welfare losses (especially by raising consumer prices) compared to global free trade; hence need for WTO to coordinate reductions in barriers

101	**Infant Industry Argument**	Rationale for protecting domestic firms from foreign competition until they have grown large enough to achieve the economies of scale to match rival foreign firms

Additional information:
Tariff protection enables them to establish themselves through internal growth but foreign competition is needed later to help deliver the cost reductions to keep prices down or deadweight loss will arise

102	**Common External Tariff**	A tax on a product imported into a customs union

Additional information:
Method of protection used by a customs union to keep down imports from non-members; the tariff is designed to raise the import price to the same level in each member country

103 **(Import) Quota**

A limit on the number of imported goods allowed into a country over a period of time

Additional information:
A barrier to trade (along with tariffs – no. 261) which leads to deadweight losses and higher consumer prices (but without a tariff's advantage as a revenue raiser for government); their effect is more certain than tariffs, which depend on elasticities

104 **Non Tariff Barriers**

Methods to prevent the sale of imports apart from tariffs or quotas

Additional information:
e.g. product quality controls designed to favour domestic firms, preferential buying from domestic firms by public sector

105	**Productive Efficiency**	Where goods are produced at the minimum possible average cost

Additional information:
Firms are driven to this under perfect competition: price competition drives out any firm which cannot produce at the lowest average costs; by contrast, monopoly can continue to sell at higher prices, earning super normal profits, because they are protected from competition by barriers to entry – indeed, the complacency this can induce in managers and workers can result in average costs rising further: X-inefficiency

106	**Allocative Efficiency** (Unit 3)	Where scarce inputs are used to maximise the social welfare generated: requires that price is set equal to marginal cost of production

Additional information:
Output where D curve (AR) – MC curve; (more accurately: P = marginal social cost) idea: all goods are produced which generate more benefit (= price consumer is willing to pay) than cost (MC) achieved by firms in perfect competition only (since only here: P = MR; in all other market structures the firm faces downward D = AR and even lower MR); not only is production on the PPC but the combination of goods matches consumer wants

107	**Dynamic Efficiency**	Where development of new products and harnessing of new technology is rapid over time

Additional information:
Requires competitive pressure (favouring smaller firms) and funding for research and development (favouring larger firms)

108	**X-Inefficiency**	The rise in average costs when a firm with monopoly power gets complacent about facing limited competition in a market

Additional information:
Requires shareholders to tolerate non profit maximisation; arguably, even monopolists face competitive pressure in the long run from firms seeking to develop new products to make the monopolist's ones obsolete ('creative destruction')

109	**Fixed Cost** (FC)	A cost which is independent of output in the short run

Additional information:
e.g. rent – in the short run this has to be paid whether the premises are in use or not; and it does not increase with output; in the long run the firm can close down and cease paying rent, therefore rent is variable in the long run

| 110 | **Variable Cost** (VC) | A cost which is related to output produced in the short run |

Additional information:
e.g. raw materials – as output increases, so more raw materials need paying for. If demand falls, a firm will close down immediately if their revenue does not cover variable costs but will stay in production in the short run if revenue just exceeds variable costs leaving something towards the fixed cost (rent?) bill that they are committed to paying for the short run period. Such a firm will close in the long run unless revenue covers all costs

| 111 | **Marginal Cost** (MC) | The addition to total cost from producing an extra unit of output |

Additional information:
MC = change in TC/change in Q. MC curve is U-shaped (in the short run), since diminishing marginal returns sets in after a certain output; MC curve cuts AC curve at AC minimum point (because when MC<AC, AC is pulled down, then when MC>AC, AC is pulled up); used to find output where profit is maximised (Q where MC = MR)

| 112 | **Law of Diminishing (Marginal) Returns** | The fall in marginal product as additional units of the variable factor of production are added to the fixed factors |

Additional information:
This is a phenomenon which occurs in the short run (because there is a fixed factor of production, usually land) arising because production gets overcrowded. The fall in marginal product (i.e. the addition to total output from an extra factor employed) is mirrored by the rise in marginal cost (since the extra cost of factors, e.g. wages, now gets spread over a reduced addition to output)

| 113 | **Average Cost** (AC) | The cost per unit of output |

Additional information:
AC = TC/Q. Short run AC curve is U-shaped, because of the influence of MC (and diminishing marginal returns); used to help calculate super normal profits for a given output: super normal profits = Q x (AR-AC). Long run AC curve is also U-shaped: up to a certain output size, economies of scale reduce LRAC to a minimum (at 'minimum efficient scale' of production), beyond this LRAC rises due to diseconomies of scale

| 114 | **Average Revenue** (AR) | The revenue per unit of output |

Additional information:
AR = TR/Q; AR = the demand curve; hence used to find the price for a chosen output

| 115 | **Marginal Revenue** (MR) | The addition to total revenue from producing an extra unit of output |

Additional information:
MR = change in TR/change in Q; MR = AR for perfect competition; otherwise MR curve is twice gradient of AR curve (from point where AR = MR on P axis); used to find output where profit is maximised (Quantity where MC = MR)

116	**Normal Profit** (NP)	The minimum (accounting) profit which the entrepreneur needs to stay in long term production

Additional information:
Normal profit = the opportunity cost of owner's time and financial capital. In economics this means normal profit = zero economist's profit (since opportunity costs are considered as costs to the firm)

117	**Super Normal Profit** (SNP)	Profit in excess of normal profit

Additional information:
Also known as abnormal profit; super normal profit acts as a signal for new firms to enter the market; super normal profit is the reward to the entrepreneur for risk-taking

118	**Short Run** (SR)	Period of time when at least one factor of production is fixed

Additional information:
In short run, a rise in demand can see any firm make super normal profit, however only those firms protected by barriers to entry will be able to make super normal profit into the long run; expansion in the short run leads to diminishing marginal returns (fall in efficiency since land can't expand to accommodate the increased labour or capital)

119	**Long Run** (LR)	Period of time when all factors of production are variable

Additional information:
In long run, all firms need to make at least normal profits or they will quit the industry; long run super normal profit is only possible for firms protected by barriers to entry; in long run, firms can expand all factors of production so can experience economies of scale (avoiding the short run expansion problem of diminishing marginal returns)

120	**Economy of Scale**	The gains in efficiency (fall in unit costs) from expanding the scale of production (i.e. from expanding all factors of production in the long run)

Additional information:
5 types: technical (area-volume relationships, indivisibility, large specialist machinery etc), bulk buying, financial, risk-spreading, specialisation

121	**Diseconomies of Scale**	The fall in efficiency (rise in unit costs) from expanding the scale of production (i.e. from expanding all factors of production in the long run)

Additional information:
Occurs when a firm becomes harder to manage (needing more costly bureaucracy), worker morale weakens and/or intra firm transport costs rise

Aims of the Firm

122	**Profit Maximisation**	Price and output are chosen to maximise supernormal profit

Additional information:
This delivers the best possible return to the firm's owners (shareholders); firm will stay in production in the long run only if it can make a minimum of normal profit (zero SNP); managers may pursue other goals because owners suffer from asymmetric information e.g. revenue or sales maximisation

123	**Revenue Maximisation**	Price and output are chosen to maximise total revenue

Additional information:
Output is sold so long as it adds to total revenue (up to where MR = zero); this entails lower price (and profit) than with profit maximisation; managers may choose this if their salary is linked to firm's total revenue (and shareholders must be unaware that super normal profit could be higher)

124	**Sales Maximisation**	Price and output are chosen to maximise sales volume (subject to earning a minimum profit)

Additional information:
In its extreme form output is sold so long as it adds to marginal profit (up to where AC = AR), where only normal profit is earned; this entails lower price (and profit) than with profit maximisation; managers may choose this if their salary is linked to market share; in more involved models it can mean maximum output subject to a minimum (positive) level of super normal profit, if shareholders expect managers to deliver stronger profits

125	**Satisficing**	Managers aim to make a satisfactory profit (anything at or above a minimum level)

Additional information:
Managers of firms with monopoly power therefore have a range of possible strategies and can afford not to profit maximise; the minimum must be at least normal profit (= zero super normal profit)

Market Structures

126	**Perfect Competition**	Market structure where there are very many (an infinite number of) buyers and sellers such that no individual can buy or sell at any price other than the 'going price'

Additional information:
Assumptions: no barriers, homogeneous product, perfect knowledge, zero transport costs etc.; long run equilibrium here ensures maximum productive and allocative efficiency

| 127 **Monopoly** | A single seller in the market or industry. (Competition Commission criteria: firm with over 25% of market share)

Additional information:
Would maximise profits by restricting output to the market (raising price); this reduces consumer surplus more than producer surplus gained (net deadweight loss). Monopoly firms can earn super normal profits in the long run because they are protected by barriers to entry; however these profits act as a powerful incentive for other firms to invent a substitute product, protected by a patent, which destroys monopoly power in the original product's market ('creative destruction'). This may impose discipline on monopoly to innovate and cut costs |
|---|---|
| 128 **Monopolistic Competition** | An industry with a large number of sellers each selling goods which are close but not perfect substitutes

Additional information:
Form of imperfect competition (i.e. the range of market structures between monopoly (one seller) and perfect competition (infinite sellers); here there is some product differentiation but no significant barriers to entry, hence only normal profits are earned in the long run; production is neither productively or allocatively efficient |
| 129 **Concentration Ratio** | The market share of the largest (specified number of) firms in an industry

Additional Information:
Can vary the number of leading firms involved: e.g. the 3 firm concentration ratio is the market share of the largest 3 firms; can use data for share of market or employment within the industry; a 'highly concentrated' market (high concentration ratio) is where the dominant firms have considerable monopoly power (e.g. in oligopoly) and collusion is easier: 'less competitive' |
| 130 **Oligopoly** | A market dominated by a few firms

Additional information:
Usually recognised by a high concentration ratio (e.g. over 50% for a 5 firm concentration ratio); form of imperfect competition; additional characteristics: high barriers to entry (e.g. branding), high degree of interdependence between firms; very common market structure featuring: price rigidity, heavy branding (non-price competition) and occasional price wars; kinked demand curve and Game Theory explain such behaviour; firms can earn super normal profits in long run (due to barriers) |

Basic Applied Theory of the Firm

| 131 | **Kinked Demand Curve** | Demand curve facing an oligopolist which is relatively price elastic if price is raised but relatively price inelastic if price is reduced |

Additional information:
Model developed in 1930s by Sweezy (US), Hall and Hitch (UK); assumes firm's pricing decision would be matched by rivals only if price is cut; creates vertical marginal revenue curve at the original output level which means marginal cost can shift without changing profit maximising price: hence explaining price rigidity in oligopoly; criticisms: branding makes top part of demand curve less elastic; can't explain price wars (unlike Game Theory)

| 132 | **Contestable Market** | An industry where there are no significant barriers to entry or exit (no sunk costs) |

Additional information:
Only normal profits may be earned in the long run; any super normal profits in the short run will attract new firms whose output will push down market price and profits in long run

| 133 | **Sunk Cost** | A cost which cannot be recouped on exiting the industry |

Additional information:
e.g. advertising, anything which cannot be sold second hand (old promotional literature etc.)

| 134 | **Merger** | Joining of two previously separate firms into one |

Additional information:
4 types: 1. horizontal (same industry, same stage of production), 2. vertical (same industry, different stage of production): a. backward (buy supplier), b. forward (e.g. buy retailer), 3. lateral (related industries), 4. conglomerate (unrelated industries); source of external growth (quicker than growing internally by reinvesting profits etc. but raises competition issues, especially when horizontal)

Strategies of the Firm

| 135 | **Price Discrimination** | Where a firm sells identical products at different prices to different buyers for reasons other than differing cost of supply |

Additional information:
Conditions necessary: 1. firm has some monopoly power, 2. the market (buyers) can be separated (to prevent resale), 3. each market has a different price elasticity of demand, 4. the cost of separating the markets must not exceed the extra revenue from charging different prices; 3 types: 1st degree ('perfect') – selling each good at highest possible price to each individual buyer; 2nd degree ('excess capacity pricing') – selling at a high initial price then dropping price to sell off any unsold goods; 3rd degree – splitting the market according to elasticity of demand

136	**Non Price Competition**	Where firms attempt to make more profit without cutting price

Additional information:
Methods include: i. branding (promoting a product to appeal to a certain consumer sub-group so they will remain customer-loyal even after price rises), ii. research and development (designing improvements to existing products), iii. product diversification (marketing a large range of brands of a single product (e.g. soap powder) to make it harder for a new entrant to attract customers who decide to try something new); usually associated with raising barriers to entry

137	**Predatory Pricing**	A short run strategy where a firm undercuts rivals on price to below cost (likely to initiate a price war)

Additional information:
In long run, smaller firm must exit the market and bigger firm can return to higher prices than they started with (having gained monopoly power); may spark off a short run price war

138	**Limit Pricing**	Where existing firms attempt to prevent new entry by pricing low so that new entrants will not make normal profits

Additional information:
Limit pricing allows existing firms to make a little super normal profit; it may be a form of long run profit maximisation; it acts as a barrier to entry

139	**Cost Plus Pricing**	Where firms set price at average cost plus a profit margin, without explicit reference to estimated demand curve

Additional information:
This is a simple pricing method that does not require managers to estimate where the demand curve (revenue curves) for their product lies; mark up margins will be lower if firms face greater competitive pressure; if firms sell out fast at the price they set, they can either produce more output or raise profit margin

140	**Collusion**	Where firms agree not to compete on price

Additional information:
A feature of oligopoly, where firms can boost profit by agreeing to raise price or restrict output together, thereby acting as if they are a monopoly supplier; it is considered anti-competitive by the Competition Authorities; 3 forms: i. a cartel formally organises collusion, ii. collusion usually implies informal agreements, iii. tacit collusion is the hardest to combat being the undocumented acceptance between rival firms not to compete hard on price (it may involve price leadership, where a dominant firm sets the price for rivals to copy)

141 **Market for Corporate Control**

The competition for control of companies through takeovers

Additional information:
Ensures that shareholder value is maximised; if dividends fall, share values will fall making the company easier to buy a controlling share in, then hostile bidder removes old management with new one to reverse the decline (raising company value for bidder); If Competition authorities make takeovers more difficult (protecting against higher concentration ratios), this process can't work

142 **Privatisation**

Broad definition: the increased use of market forces in markets previously dominated by state planning.
Narrow definition: the sale of state owned industries to the private sector

Additional information:
First major privatisation was BT in 1984; next 10 years saw most nationalised industries sold off (BR in 1994); copied abroad; a supply side policy since it increases competition

143 **Deregulation**

Removal of government regulations to allow the entry of private sector firms to compete in a market

Additional information:
Part of the process of privatisation which gathered pace after 1984 in UK and most other countries; in UK banking and transport sectors have seen a lot of deregulation recently e.g. private bus operators can now offer competition on bus routes outside London and High Street banks can offer mortgages in competition with the traditional Building Societies; expected advantages included greater pressure to cut costs and lower prices but market failures may be more likely

144 **Compulsory Competitive Tendering** (CCT)

Policy whereby government authorities invite private firms to bid for delivering publicly-funded projects and award the contract to the bidder offering the best value for the taxpayer

Additional information:
Conservative policy from 1980s in UK; designed for building large projects like hospitals or sports centres; expected to generate more innovative project designs with greater efficiency, benefiting from the incentives of competition

| 145 | **Regulator** | Government agent responsible for setting maximum prices and ensuring against abuse of monopoly power by those companies who face limited competition in product markets |

Additional information:
e.g. Regulators for the privatised utilities (natural monopolies): OFGAS, OFTEL etc. Note: natural monopolies have huge economies of scale (regional distribution network – pipelines?) hence falling LRAC. This means they are most efficient as a regional monopoly but need regulation to prevent exploitative pricing. $P = MC$ implies loss so Regulator can order $P = AC$ as a compromise (RPI – x formula governs price over a set period; firm can earn super normal profits only by making efficiency cuts of more than x%, implying a real price cut)

| 146 | **Regulatory Capture** | Where a regulated firm achieves softer regulation |

Additional information:
Firm persuades the Regulator that its costs are higher than they are, or that prospects for profitability are lower than they really are; the Regulator may tend to forget his job is to protect consumers by simulating competitive pressure because he is overexposed to the firm's problems, or he may weaken to corporate hospitality or simply fail to uncover the firm's real financial position (due to asymmetric information)

| 147 | **Multinational Companies** (MNC) | Large company with production based in several different countries |

Additional information:
e.g. General Motors, Exxon (Esso)

| 148 | **Private Finance Initiative** (PFI) | Rules allowing UK public services to be partially funded by private sector firms |

Additional information:
Introduced in 1992 to increase investment in public services without costing taxpayers' money; government departments can set up a contract for the private firm to design, build, finance or run a public service facility like a medical centre

| 149 | **Competition Policy** | Government efforts to ensure firms do not exploit monopoly power |

Additional information:
UK firms are subject to investigation by O.F.T., UK Competition Commission and an EU body (who can investigate monopolies – firms over 25% market share, mergers and anti-competitive practices like collusion)

150 **Labour Market**	The institutional arrangements whereby employment (i.e. filled job vacancies) and conditions of work (including wages) are agreed between workers (who supply their labour) and employers (who demand it)

Additional information:
Major determinant of income distribution in society; firms compete with each other to get the most productive workers at lowest possible wages, workers compete with each other to get the best paid jobs

151 **Human Capital**	The ability of workers to add value to production

Additional information:
A way of describing the factor of production labour which likens it to capital; human capital is generally owned by the workers themselves who exchange the flow of goods and services they can produce for wages/salaries; it relates to the physical and mental skills of the individual worker and is increased by training and education; spending by workers on courses may then be justified by higher earnings later, like ordinary investment in capital

152 **Marginal Revenue Product** (MRP)	The addition to total revenue from employing an extra worker

Additional information:
MRP curve = demand for labour curve (shows the maximum wage a firm would be prepared to pay for the worker)

153 **Derived Demand for Labour**	Labour is only demanded (by employers) because of the output it can produce and not because firms want workers in their own right

Additional information:
e.g. Manchester United pay Wayne Rooney a huge salary (i.e. very high demand) because he brings the club enormous revenue (higher gate receipts, more shirt sales etc.). It is a hard headed calculation rather than an expression of how the Directors personally enjoy watching his football

154 **Elasticity of Demand for Labour**	The responsiveness of demand for labour to a change in wage (ceteris paribus)

Additional information:
Equals % change in demand for labour/% change in wage; determinants:
1. PeD of labour's product, 2. wage bill as % of firm's cost, 3. ease of substituting capital for labour

155	**Productivity**	Output per factor input

Additional information:
e.g. labour productivity – output/man hour; capital productivity – output/machine; total factor productivity = a weighted average of labour and capital productivity (weights reflect the value of each factor used)

156	**Unit Labour Costs**	Labour costs per unit of output

Additional information:
Crudely: wage bill divided by total output; this is a key indicator of a country's competitiveness: if output growth can outpace growth in the total wage bill then unit labour cost (ULC) will fall; this should enable the goods to get more price competitive, provided the exchange rate does not strengthen; increased labour productivity won't result in lower ULC if wages rise at a faster rate

157	**Income Effect (and Supply of Labour)**	The increased demand for leisure (fall in supply of labour) by an individual worker as wage rates rise because workers regard leisure as a normal good to be enjoyed more as they earn more

Additional information:
This effect causes the 'backward bend' in the supply curve of labour of an individual worker (once wage rises above a critical level); hence any cut in marginal tax rate here will reduce hours worked (contrary to the government's expectations of this 'supply side policy'); however, most workers don't hit their 'backward bend' until wages rise far above market levels (exceptions: GAP year students, the very rich?)

158	**Substitution Effect (and Supply of Labour)**	The fall in demand for leisure (increased supply of labour) by an individual worker as wage rates rise because leisure becomes more expensive in terms of opportunity cost (wage foregone)

Additional information:
This effect dominates the income effect for most workers, producing the upward sloping supply curve for the individual worker; its dominance ensures that cutting marginal tax rate is an effective supply side policy, since workers respond to the higher incentive to work

159	**Elasticity of Supply of Labour**	The responsiveness of supply of labour to a change in wage (ceteris paribus)

Additional information:
Equals % change in supply of labour/% change in wage; determinants:
1. time (longer means more workers can offer themselves), 2. education/skill required (high skill jobs require lengthy training, so low pool of workers to recruit from), 3. geographical barriers (the further labour has to travel, the smaller the pool of potential workers) 4. social, language and cultural ties (jobs in different regions are not so attractive)

160	**Transfer Earnings**	The minimum payment which must be paid to keep a factor of production in its current use

Additional information:
e.g. the minimum weekly wage which Manchester United have to pay to keep Wayne Rooney at the club (which may be lower than the wages offered by a rival club, if Rooney feels there are significant non-pecuniary benefits from staying at Man. Utd e.g. a better chance of winning medals etc.); transfer earnings to a factor are shown as the area beneath the supply curve

161	**Economic Rent**	Any surplus payment above that which is necessary to keep a factor of production in its current use

Additional information:
By definition, labour's earnings are transfer earnings plus economic rent; if market wages are driven up by high demand for labour then workers will draw wage income above that necessary to keep them in that job; economic rent is shown as the area above the supply curve of labour up to the market wage; economic rent to labour is the equivalent of supernormal profits to the entrepreneur, it encourages labour to move into those jobs; if barriers to entry exist (like natural ability), economic rent can be earned into the long run

162	**Monopsony**	Single buyer in a market

Additional information:
e.g. nurses face a buyer for their labour (NHS – the government) which has very high monopsony power; only a small private health sector offers any competition to the NHS as an employer; this enables NHS to keep wages artificially low. In product markets, the major Supermarkets have monopsony power over the very many farmers who sell fresh food

163	**Trade Unions**	An organisation of workers financed by membership fees which aims to further the interests of its members e.g. negotiating with management to improve wages and working conditions (a trade union may be a monopoly seller of labour)

Additional information:
Its power to threaten strike action in pursuit of its aims can damage the competitiveness of the firm or macro economy via the establishment of a wage-price spiral; however, a trade union can also improve industrial efficiency by forcing wages up to competitive levels when workers face a monopsony employer; will cause job losses in an otherwise competitive labour market (see: supply side policy, 92)

164	**National Collective Bargaining**	Where trade unions negotiate for wages and working conditions which must apply to its workers throughout the country

Additional information:
Recent movement towards local collective bargaining or even individual wage bargaining is more likely to reduce unemployment (a supply side development); problem of national collective bargaining is that firms in rich regions can't raise wage to attract enough workers; in poor ones, excess labour at the national wage means jobs could be created if wages were allowed to fall

165	**Performance Related Pay** (PRP)	Where workers are paid in proportion to the revenue they bring to their employer

Additional information:
Acts as a powerful incentive to work, raising both demand and supply of labour, but can be difficult to implement if an individual's performance is hard to measure e.g. in many service industries

166	**Population of Working Age**	In UK: males aged 16-65, females 16-60 (i.e. school leaving age to retirement age)

Additional information:
Approximate figures for UK (2000): total population = 60.5m (19% under 18, 19% over retirement age, Population of Working Age = 37.7m); state pension age for women will rise gradually from age 60 to 65 from 2010 to 2020.

167	**Workforce**	All those of working age either in paid jobs or seeking them

Additional information:
Workforce = labour force = economically active

168	**Participation Rate**	Proportion of those of working age who are in paid jobs or seeking them

Additional information:
Includes unemployed, excludes housewives and students! Participation rate = economic activity rate

169	**National Minimum Wage** (NMW)	A floor below which wages cannot legally fall

Additional information:
Introduced in April 1999 in UK at £3.60 per hour for the over 21s (£3 for 18-20); £5.52 per hour for over 21s in 2008; arguably helps reduce inequality for those who don't lose their job; but job losses may not occur in monopsony labour markets (NHS?) or where 'shock', morale etc effects shift demand for labour; may not target impoverished very well

| 170 | **Flexible Labour Market** | A competitive (macro) labour market in which employers and workers are free to negotiate market wages and conditions of work, in which workers are adaptable to the labour needs of firms and firms are adaptable to workers' needs |

Additional information:
This involves: 1. no distortions to the labour markets e.g. national minimum wages, trade unions, monopsony employer, 2. labour which is occupationally and geographically mobile (e.g. capable of retraining), 3. employers who can offer part-time work etc to enable workers (usually female) to balance child care with paid work

| 171 | **Working Time Directive** (WTD) | Regulation setting a maximum number of hours per week an employer can insist his employees work |

Additional information:
Part of the EU's Social Chapter which UK adheres to; in UK the maximum is 48 hours a week, although workers can sign away this right and not all workers are covered (e.g. doctors)

| 172 | **Social Chapter** | Section of the Maastricht Treaty which commits European Union countries to guarantee certain legal rights of workers in the labour market |

Additional information:
Covers rights to equal treatment of men and women, union membership, fair pay, health and safety at work; UK Government signed in 1997, after having negotiated an 'opt out' clause in 1991; justifies the National Minimum Wage and Working Time Directive; creates a level playing field within EU where all workers get protection, helping labour mobility, and firms can't relocate to source cheaper labour; but institutionalises higher labour costs, making workers less flexible

| 173 | **New Deal** | New Labour's policy to combat long term unemployment: after a period of assisted job search, an unemployed person is guaranteed some form of paid work (voluntary work or subsidised employment) or training |

Additional information:
Launched in April 1998 for the 18-24 age group, it now covers many other unemployed; the rationale is that periods of unemployment diminish human capital because people lose self esteem and skills through lack of practice; benefit is withdrawn if person refuses to cooperate; New Deal is a supply side policy to make labour market more flexible

174 **Income** (Y) Money earned over a period of time

Additional information:
e.g. £100 per week: a flow concept; income may come from earned (wages) or unearned (dividends, inheritance) sources; gross (pre tax) or net (post tax) or disposable (post tax and cash state benefits, sometimes post mortgage repayments) or final (disposable plus state benefits in kind, like state healthcare or education which is free at the point of use); income is a key determinant of other flow concepts like consumption

175 **Wealth** (W) The value of an individual's assets at a point in time

Additional information:
A stock concept e.g. £10,000 now (not per period of time); can be physical (house value) or monetary (share value); a key determinant of flow concepts like consumption

176 **Horizontal Equity** The equal treatment of people in the same circumstances

Additional information:
e.g. government charging same income tax to all people earning the same income; uncontroversial

177 **Vertical Equity** The notion which can be used to justify taxing richer people more to bring about greater 'fairness'

Additional information:
Highly controversial bit of normative economics; used to justify redistribution of income from rich to poor, sometimes on the grounds of giving poorer people equality of opportunity

178 **Lorenz Curve** Graphical representation of inequality: cumulative shares of (e.g.) income are plotted against cumulative shares of the population

Additional information:
e.g. the share of total income earned by the poorest 10% is plotted as a point; more curved = more unequal distribution

179 **Gini Coefficient** A statistical measure of inequality; on Lorenz curve diagram, Gini coefficient = area between line of equality and Lorenz curve/whole area under line of equality

Additional information:
Values: 0 = perfect equality, 1 = maximum inequality; Gini coefficients have been rising since 1979 in UK for income and wealth inequality

180	**Decile**	10% of the population of a group

Additional information:
Usually used for (UK) income distribution: the lowest decile is the poorest 10% (in UK)

181	**Quintile**	20% of the population of a group

Additional information:
Usually used for (UK) income distribution: the lowest quintile is the poorest 20% (in UK)

182	**Absolute Poverty**	A state where a household or person is unable to purchase the basic necessities to sustain a civilised life

Additional information:
Eradicating this is considered a desirable goal for most industrialised economies and is certainly achievable in all but the poorest economies. Its level is related to human needs and involves having enough food not to be constantly hungry i.e. more than achieving mere biological survival, having somewhere to live (not just access to a soup kitchen by night) etc.

183	**Relative Poverty**	A state where a household or person is significantly poorer than the average for the rest of society

Additional information:
Usually set at less than 50% (or 40%) of median earnings. Eradicating it is achievable with enough redistribution of income (so that the poorest are all between 50-100% of median earnings) but it is considered less serious than absolute poverty. But feelings of alienation from society may lead to unhappiness, illness and crime

184	**Poverty Trap**	The disincentive to work when someone on benefits faces a very high effective marginal rate of tax if they work harder

Additional information:
This can arise when starting income tax is relatively high and benefits are suddenly withdrawn when someone starts work or earns more in work. Recent UK government policy e.g. Working Families Tax Credit has been aimed at removing poverty traps as part of supply side policy

185	**Replacement Ratio**	The ratio of unemployment benefits to average earnings

Additional information:
If the replacement ratio is high, this reduces the incentive to take up paid employment e.g. if the replacement ratio is close to or above 100% this acts as an unemployment trap, an effective poverty trap; reducing the replacement ratio is therefore a supply side policy which has been followed in UK since 1980

186	**Means Tested Benefits**	Benefits which are only paid to households who can prove they are poor

Additional information:
e.g. certain housing benefits; such benefits are well targeted at the poor (justified by vertical equity) but take-up may be low if households object to revealing such information; by contrast, universal benefits like state pensions and child benefit are paid at the same rate to recipients regardless of current income (on grounds of horizontal equity)

187	**Demographic Timebomb**	The negative effects of the ageing of the populations in the industrialised world

Additional information:
Causes: 1. falling birth rates; 2. increased life expectancy; 3. early retirement. Effects: rising dependency ratio (= population of non working age/population of working age) leading to increased pension spending by government. Possible solutions: raise taxes on workers, reduce pension rates, raise retirement age, move from taxpayer funded to private or (Stock market) funded pensions

188	**Productive Efficiency**	Where goods are produced at the minimum possible average cost

Additional information:
Firms are driven to this under perfect competition: price competition drives out any firm which cannot produce at the lowest average costs; by contrast, monopoly can continue to sell at higher prices, earning super normal profits, because they are protected from competition by barriers to entry – indeed, the complacency this can induce in managers and workers can result in average costs rising further: X-inefficiency

189	**Allocative Efficiency** (Unit 3)	Where scarce inputs are used to maximise the social welfare generated: requires that price is set equal to marginal cost of production

Additional information:
Output where D curve (AR) = MC curve; (more accurately: P = marginal social cost) idea: all goods are produced which generate more benefit (= price consumer is willing to pay) than cost (MC) achieved by firms in perfect competition only (since only here: P = MR; in all other market structures the firm faces downward D = AR and even lower MR); not only is production on the PPC but the combination of goods matches consumer wants

190	**Dynamic Efficiency**	Where development of new products and harnessing of new technology is rapid over time

Additional information:
Requires competitive pressure (favouring smaller firms) and funding for research and development (favouring larger firms)

191	**X-Inefficiency**	The rise in average costs when a firm with monopoly power gets complacent about facing limited competition in a market

Additional information:
Requires shareholders to tolerate non profit maximisation; arguably, even monopolists face competitive pressure in the long run from firms seeking to develop new products to make the monopolist's ones obsolete ('creative destruction')

192	**Fixed Cost** (FC)	A cost which is independent of output in the short run

Additional information:
e.g. rent – in the short run this has to be paid whether the premises are in use or not; and it does not increase with output; in the long run the firm can close down and cease paying rent, therefore rent is variable in the long run

193	**Variable Cost** (VC)	A cost which is related to output produced in the short run

Additional information:
e.g. raw materials – as output increases, so more raw materials need paying for. If demand falls, a firm will close down immediately if their revenue does not cover variable costs but will stay in production in the short run if revenue just exceeds variable costs leaving something towards the fixed cost (rent?) bill that they are committed to paying for the short run period. Such a firm will close in the long run unless revenue covers all costs

194	**Marginal Cost** (MC)	The addition to total cost from producing an extra unit of output

Additional information:
MC = change in TC/change in Q. MC curve is U-shaped (in the short run), since diminishing marginal returns sets in after a certain output; MC curve cuts AC curve at AC minimum point (because when MC<AC, AC is pulled down, then when MC>AC, AC is pulled up); used to find output where profit is maximised (Q where MC = MR)

195	**Law of Diminishing (Marginal) Returns**	The fall in marginal product as additional units of the variable factor of production are added to the fixed factors

Additional information:
This is a phenomenon which occurs in the short run (because there is a fixed factor of production, usually land) arising because production gets overcrowded. The fall in marginal product (i.e. the addition to total output from an extra factor employed) is mirrored by the rise in marginal cost (since the extra cost of factors, e.g. wages, now gets spread over a reduced addition to output)

196	**Average Cost** (AC)	The cost per unit of output

Additional information:
AC = TC/Q. Short run AC curve is U-shaped, because of the influence of MC (and diminishing marginal returns); used to help calculate super normal profits for a given output: super normal profits = Q x (AR-AC). Long run AC curve is also U-shaped: up to a certain output size, economies of scale reduce LRAC to a minimum (at 'minimum efficient scale' of production), beyond this LRAC rises due to diseconomies of scale

197	**Average Revenue** (AR)	The revenue per unit of output

Additional information:
AR = TR/Q; AR = the demand curve; hence used to find the price for a chosen output

198	**Marginal Revenue** (MR)	The addition to total revenue from producing an extra unit of output

Additional information:
MR = change in TR/change in Q; MR = AR for perfect competition; otherwise MR curve is twice gradient of AR curve (from point where AR = MR on P axis); used to find output where profit is maximised (Quantity where MC = MR)

199	**Normal Profit** (NP)	The minimum (accounting) profit which the entrepreneur needs to stay in long term production
		Additional information: Normal profit = the opportunity cost of owner's time and financial capital. In economics this means normal profit = zero economist's profit (since opportunity costs are considered as costs to the firm)
200	**Super Normal Profit** (SNP)	Profit in excess of normal profit
		Additional information: Also known as abnormal profit; super normal profit acts as a signal for new firms to enter the market; super normal profit is the reward to the entrepreneur for risk-taking
201	**Short Run** (SR)	Period of time when at least one factor of production is fixed
		Additional information: In short run, a rise in demand can see any firm make super normal profit, however only those firms protected by barriers to entry will be able to make super normal profit into the long run; expansion in the short run leads to diminishing marginal returns (fall in efficiency since land can't expand to accommodate the increased labour or capital)
202	**Long Run** (LR)	Period of time when all factors of production are variable
		Additional information: In long run, all firms need to make at least normal profits or they will quit the industry; long run super normal profit is only possible for firms protected by barriers to entry; in long run, firms can expand all factors of production so can experience economies of scale (avoiding the short run expansion problem of diminishing marginal returns)
203	**Economy of Scale**	The gains in efficiency (fall in unit costs) from expanding the scale of production (i.e. from expanding all factors of production in the long run)
		Additional information: 5 types: technical (area-volume relationships, indivisibility, large specialist machinery etc), bulk buying, financial, risk-spreading, specialisation
204	**Diseconomies of Scale**	The fall in efficiency (rise in unit costs) from expanding the scale of production (i.e. from expanding all factors of production in the long run)
		Additional information: Occurs when a firm becomes harder to manage (needing more costly bureaucracy), worker morale weakens and/or intra firm transport costs rise

Section B:		**Aims of the Firm**

205 Profit Maximisation

Price and output are chosen to maximise supernormal profit

Additional information:
This delivers the best possible return to the firm's owners (shareholders); firm will stay in production in the long run only if it can make a minimum of normal profit (zero SNP); managers may pursue other goals because owners suffer from asymmetric information e.g. revenue or sales maximisation

206 Revenue Maximisation

Price and output are chosen to maximise total revenue

Additional information:
Output is sold so long as it adds to total revenue (up to where MR = zero); this entails lower price (and profit) than with profit maximisation; managers may choose this if their salary is linked to firm's total revenue (and shareholders must be unaware that super normal profit could be higher)

207 Sales Maximisation

Price and output are chosen to maximise sales volume (subject to earning a minimum profit)

Additional information:
In its extreme form output is sold so long as it adds to marginal profit (up to where AC = AR), where only normal profit is earned; this entails lower price (and profit) than with profit maximisation; managers may choose this if their salary is linked to market share; in more involved models it can mean maximum output subject to a minimum (positive) level of super normal profit, if shareholders expect managers to deliver stronger profits

208 Satisficing

Managers aim to make a satisfactory profit (anything at or above a minimum level)

Additional information:
Managers of firms with monopoly power therefore have a range of possible strategies and can afford not to profit maximise; the minimum must be at least normal profit (= zero super normal profit)

Section C:		**Market Structures**

209 Perfect Competition

Market structure where there are very many (an infinite number of) buyers and sellers such that no individual can buy or sell at any price other than the 'going price'

Additional information:
Assumptions: no barriers, homogeneous product, perfect knowledge, zero transport costs etc.; long run equilibrium here ensures maximum productive and allocative efficiency

210	**Monopoly**	A single seller in the market or industry. (Competition Commission criteria: firm with over 25% of market share)

Additional information:
Would maximise profits by restricting output to the market (raising price); this reduces consumer surplus more than producer surplus gained (net deadweight loss). Monopoly firms can earn super normal profits in the long run because they are protected by barriers to entry; however these profits act as a powerful incentive for other firms to invent a substitute product, protected by a patent, which destroys monopoly power in the original product's market ('creative destruction'). This may impose discipline on monopoly to innovate and cut costs

211	**Monopolistic Competition**	An industry with a large number of sellers each selling goods which are close but not perfect substitutes

Additional information:
Form of imperfect competition (i.e. the range of market structures between monopoly (one seller) and perfect competition (infinite sellers); here there is some product differentiation but no significant barriers to entry, hence only normal profits are earned in the long run; production is neither productively or allocatively efficient

212	**Concentration Ratio**	The market share of the largest (specified number of) firms in an industry

Additional information:
Can vary the number of leading firms involved: e.g. the 3 firm concentration ratio is the market share of the largest 3 firms; can use data for share of market or employment within the industry; a 'highly concentrated' market (high concentration ratio) is where the dominant firms have considerable monopoly power (e.g. in oligopoly) and collusion is easier: 'less competitive'

213	**Oligopoly**	A market dominated by a few firms

Additional information:
Usually recognised by a high concentration ratio (e.g. over 50% for a 5 firm concentration ratio); form of imperfect competition; additional characteristics: high barriers to entry (e.g. branding), high degree of interdependence between firms; very common market structure featuring: price rigidity, heavy branding (non-price competition) and occasional price wars; kinked demand curve and Game Theory explain such behaviour; firms can earn super normal profits in long run (due to barriers)

	Section D:	**Basic Applied Theory of the Firm**

214 Kinked Demand Curve

Demand curve facing an oligopolist which is relatively price elastic if price is raised but relatively price inelastic if price is reduced

Additional information:
Model developed in 1930s by Sweezy (US), Hall and Hitch (UK); assumes firm's pricing decision would be matched by rivals only if price is cut; creates vertical marginal revenue curve at the original output level which means marginal cost can shift without changing profit maximising price: hence explaining price rigidity in oligopoly; criticisms: branding makes top part of demand curve less elastic; can't explain price wars (unlike Game Theory)

215 Contestable Market

An industry where there are no significant barriers to entry or exit (no sunk costs)

Additional information:
Only normal profits may be earned in the long run; any super normal profits in the short run will attract new firms whose output will push down market price and profits in long run

216 Sunk Cost

A cost which cannot be recouped on exiting the industry

Additional information:
e.g. advertising, anything which cannot be sold second hand (old promotional literature etc.)

217 Merger

Joining of two previously separate firms into one

Additional information:
4 types: 1. horizontal (same industry, same stage of production), 2. vertical (same industry, different stage of production): a. backward (buy supplier), b. forward (e.g. buy retailer), 3. lateral (related industries), 4. conglomerate (unrelated industries); source of external growth (quicker than growing internally by reinvesting profits etc. but raises competition issues, especially when horizontal)

	Section E:	**Strategies of the Firm**

218 Price Discrimination

Where a firm sells identical products at different prices to different buyers for reasons other than differing cost of supply

Additional information:
Conditions necessary: 1. firm has some monopoly power, 2. the market (buyers) can be separated (to prevent resale), 3. each market has a different price elasticity of demand, 4. the cost of separating the markets must not exceed the extra revenue from charging different prices; 3 types: 1st degree ('perfect') – selling each good at highest possible price to each individual buyer; 2nd degree ('excess capacity pricing') – selling at a high initial price then dropping price to sell off any unsold goods; 3rd degree – splitting the market according to elasticity of demand

219	**Non Price Competition**	Where firms attempt to make more profit without cutting price

Additional information:
Methods include: i. branding (promoting a product to appeal to a certain consumer sub-group so they will remain customer-loyal even after price rises), ii. research and development (designing improvements to existing products), iii. product diversification (marketing a large range of brands of a single product (e.g. soap powder) to make it harder for a new entrant to attract customers who decide to try something new); usually associated with raising barriers to entry

220	**Predatory Pricing**	A short run strategy where a firm undercuts rivals on price to below cost (likely to initiate a price war)

Additional information:
In long run, smaller firm must exit the market and bigger firm can return to higher prices than they started with (having gained monopoly power); may spark off a short run price war

221	**Limit Pricing**	Where existing firms attempt to prevent new entry by pricing low so that new entrants will not make normal profits

Additional information:
Limit pricing allows existing firms to make a little super normal profit; it may be a form of long run profit maximisation; it acts as a barrier to entry

222	**Cost Plus Pricing**	Where firms set price at average cost plus a profit margin, without explicit reference to estimated demand curve

Additional information:
This is a simple pricing method that does not require managers to estimate where the demand curve (revenue curves) for their product lies; mark up margins will be lower if firms face greater competitive pressure; if firms sell out fast at the price they set, they can either produce more output or raise profit margin

223	**Collusion**	Where firms agree not to compete on price

Additional information:
A feature of oligopoly, where firms can boost profit by agreeing to raise price or restrict output together, thereby acting as if they are a monopoly supplier; it is considered anti-competitive by the Competition Authorities; 3 forms: i. a cartel formally organises collusion, ii. collusion usually implies informal agreements, iii. tacit collusion is the hardest to combat being the undocumented acceptance between rival firms not to compete hard on price (it may involve price leadership, where a dominant firm sets the price for rivals to copy)

224	**Market for Corporate Control**	The competition for control of companies through takeovers

Additional information:
Ensures that shareholder value is maximised; if dividends fall, share values will fall making the company easier to buy a controlling share in, then hostile bidder removes old management with new one to reverse the decline (raising company value for bidder); if Competition authorities make takeovers more difficult (protecting against higher concentration ratios), this process can't work

225	**Privatisation**	Broad definition: the increased use of market forces in markets previously dominated by state planning. Narrow definition: the sale of state owned industries to the private sector

Additional information:
First major privatisation was BT in 1984; next 10 years saw most nationalised industries sold off (BR in 1994); copied abroad; a supply side policy since it increases competition

226	**Deregulation**	Removal of government regulations to allow the entry of private sector firms to compete in a market

Additional information:
Part of the process of privatisation which gathered pace after 1984 in UK and most other countries; in UK banking and transport sectors have seen a lot of deregulation recently e.g. private bus operators can now offer competition on bus routes outside London and High Street banks can offer mortgages in competition with the traditional Building Societies; expected advantages included greater pressure to cut costs and lower prices but market failures may be more likely

227	**Compulsory Competitive Tendering** (CCT)	Policy whereby government authorities invite private firms to bid for delivering publicly-funded projects and award the contract to the bidder offering the best value for the taxpayer

Additional information:
Conservative policy from 1980s in UK; designed for building large projects like hospitals or sports centres; expected to generate more innovative project designs with greater efficiency, benefiting from the incentives of competition

| 228 | **Regulator** | Government agent responsible for setting maximum prices and ensuring against abuse of monopoly power by those companies who face limited competition in product markets |

Additional information:
e.g. Regulators for the privatised utilities (natural monopolies): OFGAS, OFTEL etc. Note: natural monopolies have huge economies of scale (regional distribution network – pipelines?) hence falling LRAC. This means they are most efficient as a regional monopoly but need regulation to prevent exploitative pricing. $P = MC$ implies loss so Regulator can order $P = AC$ as a compromise (RPI – x formula governs price over a set period; firm can earn super normal profits only by making efficiency cuts of more than x%, implying a real price cut)

| 229 | **Regulatory Capture** | Where a regulated firm achieves softer regulation |

Additional information:
Firm persuades the Regulator that its costs are higher than they are, or that prospects for profitability are lower than they really are; the Regulator may tend to forget his job is to protect consumers by simulating competitive pressure because he is overexposed to the firm's problems, or he may weaken to corporate hospitality or simply fail to uncover the firm's real financial position (due to asymmetric information)

| 230 | **Multinational Companies** (MNC) | Large company with production based in several different countries |

Additional information:
e.g. General Motors, Exxon (Esso)

| 231 | **Private Finance Initiative** (PFI) | Rules allowing UK public services to be partially funded by private sector firms |

Additional information:
Introduced in 1992 to increase investment in public services without costing taxpayers' money; government departments can set up a contract for the private firm to design, build, finance or run a public service facility like a medical centre

---

| 232 | **Competition Policy** | Government efforts to ensure firms do not exploit monopoly power |

Additional information:
UK firms are subject to investigation by O.F.T., UK Competition Commission and an EU body (who can investigate monopolies – firms over 25% market share, mergers and anti-competitive practices like collusion)

Transport Markets

233 Transport

The movement of people and goods via a range of different modes

Additional information:
Different modes: car, bus, rail, cycle, ship etc; provision of the infrastructure (road, rail network etc) is separate from the provision of operations (bus services, train services etc); transport involves huge public sector spending (mostly providing infrastructure) alongside huge private sector spending (private car journeys, bus/rail companies); is an arena of considerable market failure and potential for government failure

234 Derived Demand

Demand for a product (or factor of production) which is demanded only because of demand for the final product it contributes to

Additional information:
e.g. demand for transport by holidaymakers (or demand for labour by firms)

235 Natural Monopoly

Industry with cost structure dominated by huge economies of scale hence falling long run average costs

Additional information:
e.g. industries with regional distribution network like gas, water, electricity supply (but also large infrastructure projects like Channel Tunnel). Marginal costs (e.g. of electricity supply) are tiny in relation to the enormous fixed costs (e.g. of building the grid); hence as output increases the fall in average fixed costs dominates rises in average variable costs. This means they are most productively efficient run as a (regional) monopoly (to avoid wasteful duplication of competing networks) but need regulation to prevent exploitative pricing. P = MC (allocative optimum) implies loss so Regulator can order P = AC as a compromise

236 Privatisation

Broad definition: the increased use of market forces in markets previously dominated by state planning.
Narrow definition: the sale of state owned industries to the private sector

Additional information:
First major privatisation was BT in 1984; next 10 years saw most nationalised industries sold off (BR in 1994); copied abroad; a supply side policy since it increases competition

237	**Deregulation**	Removal of government regulations to allow the entry of private sector firms to compete in a market

Additional information:
Part of the process of privatisation which gathered pace after 1984 in UK and most other countries; in UK banking and transport sectors have seen a lot of doregulation recently e.g. private bus operators can now offer competition on bus routes outside London and High Street banks can offer mortgages in competition with the traditional Building Societies; expected advantages included greater pressure to cut costs and lower prices but market failures may be more likely

238	**Marginal Private Cost** (MPC)	The addition to total cost to the firm from an extra unit of production

Additional information:
Normally, MPC = the supply curve

239	**Marginal External Cost** (MEC)	The additional (external) cost suffered by the third party from an extra unit of production

Additional information:
e.g. damage to health from pollution or loss of time from road congestion

240	**Marginal Social Cost** (MSC)	The additional cost to society (i.e. firm + third party) from an extra unit of production

Additional information:
MSC = MPC + MEC

241	**Marginal Private Benefit** (MPB)	The additional benefit to the consumer from an extra unit of production

Additional information:
MPB = the demand curve

242	**Marginal External Benefit** (MEB)	The additional (external) benefit to third parties from an extra unit of production

Additional information:
e.g. 3rd parties benefit for free from another person's consumption of inoculations (less chance of disease) or education (advice given)

243	**Marginal Social Benefit** (MSB)	The additional benefit to society (i.e. consumers + third parties) from an extra unit of production

Additional information:
MSB = MPB + MEB

244	**Socially Optimal Production**	Output where allocative efficiency is maximised (i.e. MSB = MSC)

Additional information:
Maximum welfare to society is generated here; usually associated with some negative external costs (though less than under free market levels) because eliminating all external costs is very expensive

245	**Deadweight Loss**	Net welfare lost from not producing at the socially optimal production

Additional information:
Measured as excess of MSC over MSB (where overproduction occurs for negative externality) or as excess of MSB over MSC (where net social benefit is lost through underproduction); can also occur in monopoly markets and when indirect taxes are levied

246	**Optimal Tax**	Tax equal to marginal external cost (persuading profit maximising firms to choose socially optimal production)

Additional information:
Ideal solution for negative externalities (internalising the external cost) but requires accurate information and enforcement

247	**Road Pricing**	Charging drivers for the journeys they make, based on the road location, length of journey and time of day

Additional information:
Contrasts with road tax which is paid on ownership of a car; road pricing shifts the cost of driving from fixed cost to variable cost and has been proposed as a solution to the problem of road congestion since drivers otherwise do not face the marginal external costs involved in rush hour journeys; can take the form of road tolls or electronic tagging (e.g. central London congestion charge since February 2003); disadvantages: may shift traffic onto unpriced roads and is hard to set at optimal (variable) level

248	**Hypothecated Tax**	A tax which raises revenue from one source which must be spent in a specific way

Additional information:
No current examples in the UK (except perhaps TV licence fee which goes to the BBC), although many feel vehicle excise duty (road tax) ought to be spent on maintaining the road network; the advantage of hypothecating a tax is to encourage willing payment since it gives politicians less scope to spend money as they please, but others argue that government needs more flexibility

249	**Regulation**	Rules from government requiring firms to modify their production techniques, output or price

Additional information:
Crude solution to externality problem requiring government to measure the externalities and set suitable limits which are enforceable

250	**Tradable Permit**	A legal right to pollute a fixed amount which can be bought or sold between firms
		Additional information: Government establishes where the socially optimal production is and divides up the level of pollution existing here into tradable units; this is a sophisticated solution to the externality problem where reduction in output is achieved in the most cost efficient way i.e. by those firms which can most easily do so (who sell permits to the other firms within a secondary market for tradable permits)
251	**Property Right**	A legal entitlement (which can be bought or sold) to the exclusive use of a resource
		Additional information: When absent (e.g. an open common, unregulated sea fishing), individuals have little incentive not to over-exploit the resource in the short term; extending property rights is a potential solution for such market failures, but often impractical e.g. establishing property rights for road space at a particular time
252	**Quasi Public Goods**	Goods which exhibit partial non-excludability or non-rivalry
		Additional information: e.g. most UK roads can be seen as a public good but they become private goods if made excludable by road pricing schemes (e.g. tolls) and when they are rival (e.g. when congested)
253	**Integrated Transport Policy**	A national policy designed to cover all modes of transport aiming to improve the ability of society to meet their transport needs as efficiently as possible
		Additional information: In practice, this means ensuring that individual journeys work smoothly when they involve connections between road and rail etc but also that people are incentivised to make journeys as cost effectively as possible from society''s viewpoint e.g. coordinating the subsidy of bus journeys and taxation of car journeys to reduce urban congestion
254	**Sustainable Transport Policy**	A national policy that ensures that current *and future* generations can meet their transport needs as efficiently as possible
		Additional information: Given the forecasted growth in road use, this may mean taxing car journeys more heavily to build up public transportation which produces less congestion and pollution per passenger mile
255	**Cost Benefit Analysis**	Technique used to assess whether public sector projects are likely to produce net gains in welfare to society
		Additional information: Projects will only be attempted if the social benefits are expected to outweigh the social costs; as a result, government only use this for large investment projects which generate sizeable externalities e.g. building the extended Jubilee tube line; ordinary private sector projects simply proceed on the calculation of expected profit – where private benefit (revenue) exceeds private cost, which is optimal for society in the absence of market failures like externalities

256	**Trade Liberalisation**	Removal of barriers to international trade

Additional information:
Removing tariffs and non-tariff barriers to trade in goods and services in addition to allowing citizens to exchange unlimited amounts of currency in the currency markets; trade has become increasingly liberalised as globalisation has gathered pace since 1980; the result of free trade should be gains for all participants as each country begins to specialise more in production of those goods where they have a comparative advantage

257	**Globalisation**	The growing integration and interdependence of the world economy i.e. the increased international movement of output, financial capital, foreign direct investment (multinational production) and the harmonisation of consumer tastes

Additional information:
Causes: improved transport and communication, reduction in trade barriers and removal of exchange controls; motives (for FDI): siting production where costs are lowest to maximise profit, dodging tariff barriers; effects: loss of jobs in low skill-high wage industrialised economies to low wage developing world, cheaper consumer goods

258	**World Trade Organisation** (WTO)	Organisation to promote free trade and coordinate (and police) reduction in barriers to trade

Additional information:
Set up in 1995 to replace GATT (General Agreement on Tariffs and Trade)

259	**Comparative Advantage** (C/A)	The producer with the lowest opportunity cost of production (or highest output per factor of production) for a particular product

Additional information:
If persons or national economies specialise in production of the good they have a comparative advantage in, all can gain from trade

260	**Absolute Advantage** (A/A)	The producer with the ability to make the largest amount of a particular product using its factors of production

Additional information:
Having absolute advantage in production of a product does not mean specialisation in it will lead to gains from trade (see comparative advantage, 259); a producer can have absolute advantage in several products

Economic Integration

261 **Tariff**

Tax levied on an import

Additional information:
Raises price for consumers (reducing consumer surplus) but allows domestic producers to sell more in the domestic market (raising their producer surplus); leads to net welfare loss; a form of protectionism

262 **Free Trade Area (FTA)**

A group of countries which coordinate a reduction in trade barriers between themselves but do not erect a common external tariff

Additional information:
e.g. EFTA 1960 – included UK, Sweden, Denmark, Switzerland, Portugal (till joining EU); often progresses to customs union because each country has different tariff against non-members (hence lowest tariff forms gateway to goods from outside, benefiting import-export firms in that nation)

263 **Customs Union**

A group of countries with reduced trade barriers (tariffs + quotas) between members but a common external tariff against imports from outside

Additional information:
e.g. European Economic Community 1973-1992 (prior to becoming a common market: EU); this leads to trade creation (benefit) but trade diversion (cost) (see 269-270), the latter also imposing costs on non-members, who may respond with trade barriers against the customs union

264 **Common Market**

The stage of economic integration between states when barriers to capital (e.g. exchange controls) and labour mobility (e.g. visas) are removed

Additional information:
This stage naturally follows setting up of customs union; EU achieved this (Single European Market) in 1992; it can lead on to Economic and Monetary Union; common market enables efficiency gains since firms can draw on labour supply from entire union (less labour shortages build up requiring increased wage rates) and firms can borrow money more cheaply, tapping into the savings of the entire union

265 **Economic and Monetary Union (EMU)**

When a group of countries in a common market abolish national currencies to share a single currency (and therefore operate a single monetary policy for the whole union)

Additional information:
e.g. EU 12 (not UK) entered EMU in 1999 with the Euro (national currencies locked against Euro until abolition in 2002); arguments for: reduced costs, stable currency, anti inflationary; arguments against: loss of macro policy independence (interest rates, fiscal constraints) to deal with asymmetric shocks – labour must be flexible to cope

266	**Convergence Criteria**	Macro economic conditions which must be met before a country is allowed to join an Economic and Monetary Union

Additional information:
For Europe's EMU this covered: low inflation (below 2.7%, as at Jan 1998), low government budget deficit (maximum 3% GDP), low national debt (maximum 60% GDP), low long term interest rate (below 7.8%, as at Jan 1998) and exchange rate stability (for two years) against other EMU currencies; meeting these criteria should indicate that an economy is ready for EMU membership e.g. it won't need exchange rate depreciation to rescue its export sector due to excessive domestic inflation

267	**Stability and Growth Pact**	Limit placed on government budget deficit for countries belonging to the European Single Currency

Additional information:
Agreed by member countries of the European Economic and Monetary Union in June 1997; budget deficit should not exceed 3% GDP in any one year, or risk the imposition of fines; Its rationale? To prevent individual countries creating inflationary pressure by running a budget deficit (one government's fiscal laxity could raise EU inflation, bringing European Central Bank interest rate rises which would slow down the entire EMU economy)

268	**Trading Bloc**	A group of countries who form a free trade area, customs union or common market as a way to reduce trade barriers between them and raise barriers to non-members

Additional information:
e.g. European Union, NAFTA, ASEAN

269	**Trade Creation**	The welfare gains from joining a customs union

Additional information:
These derive from having reduced trade barriers with customs union members e.g. lower tariffs will enable countries to specialise more in what they have a comparative advantage in, gaining the 2 triangles of deadweight loss in the standard textbook tariff diagram

270	**Trade Diversion**	The welfare losses to a country from joining a customs union

Additional information:
These derive from having to adopt a common external tariff which may raise the price of imports from low cost producers outside the customs union e.g. rise in price of New Zealand butter when UK joined EEC in 1973

Exchange Rates and Balance of Payments

271	**Exchange Rate System**	The rules which determine how a country's exchange rate is set

Additional information:
Either: floating, dirty (semi) floating, semi fixed (e.g. Exchange Rate Mechanism), fixed or EMU

272	**Fixed Exchange Rate System**	Exchange rate is maintained at a target level by government interventions in the currency market

Additional information:
Often the target is a range e.g. ERM (UK: 1990-2). When downward pressure on Sterling exchange rate occurs (trade deficit), government buys £'s using reserves of foreign currency and/or raises interest rates to attract 'hot money' inflows (demand for £'s rises) or deflates UK economy (less imports: supply of £'s falls), hence trade deficit reversed; advantages: anti-inflationary (discipline on wages: devaluation cannot come to rescue of uncompetitive firms)

273	**Floating Exchange Rate System**	Exchange rate is freely determined by market forces (without government intervention)

Additional information:
Trade deficit causes depreciation of currency, this softens job losses in short run; despite being subject to fluctuation, in this system a currency should be immune from major speculative attack (e.g. George Soros on Sterling, 1992)

274	**Balance of Payments Disequilibrium**	Where Balance of Payments current account has a large, persistent and rising deficit (or surplus) over time

Additional information:
In the long run such a deficit can only be supported by matching inflows on the financial account (e.g. from sale of assets or borrowing) which is unsustainable

275	**Devaluation**	Fall in value of exchange rate, usually announced by government when part of a fixed exchange rate system (Note: 'depreciation' = fall in exchange rate when in floating regime)

Additional information:
Effects are to raise import prices and decrease export prices (fall in terms of trade), which gives initial impetus to export sector (though wage-price spirals can undo competitiveness); effect on balance of payments current account is only positive if Marshall Lerner condition holds

276	**Marshall Lerner Condition**	The sum of elasticity of demand for exports and imports must exceed one

Additional information:
This guarantees that a devaluation of currency will improve the trade balance on balance of payments current account. N.B. surprisingly, if each elasticity is 0.6 (inelastic) the trade balance still improves! In short run, J curve reflects low elasticities

277	**J Curve Effect**	The short term fall in Balance of Payments current account following a devaluation of the exchange rate before long run elastic demand for imports and exports leads to rise

Additional information:
Measures balance of payments current account (vertical axis) against time; in short run firms don't sell more exports because existing contracts reflect previous exchange rate therefore same volume of exports earns less as price has fallen (same for imports, in reverse)

278	**'Hot Money'**	Money in search of the highest short term rate of return available internationally

Additional information:
Such sums are moved by large financial investors into economies where rates of interest are increasing relative to others (so long as the nominal exchange rate is not depreciating at a greater rate); this adds volatility to exchange rate movements since e.g. rises in UK interest rate creates hot money inflows which drive up demand for sterling …until UK interest rates fall relatively, when the hot money flows out leading to sterling falls; unlike foreign direct investment, these flows are short term, like currency speculation

279	**'Dutch Disease'**	Where the strength of one sector of an economy drives up the exchange rate to a point where its other sectors lose competitiveness

Additional information:
Arguably one of the factors causing the UK manufacturing recession in 1980-82, when North Sea Oil created massive demand for sterling which drove up the currency so far that other export sectors, like steel and cars, suffered a major loss of price competitiveness abroad

280	**Real Exchange Rate** (Real ER)	The price of a country's goods relative to those produced abroad when expressed in a common currency

Additional information:
Measures international competitiveness (combines movement in nominal exchange rate and relative inflation). When UK's real exchange rate rises UK exports become more expensive for foreigners relative to foreign produced substitutes: i.e. less price competitive; this can occur for 2 reasons: i. UK's inflation is relatively higher than abroad ii. UK's nominal exchange rate rises. Hence, real exchange rate is the ratio of $ price of UK goods (= its £ price x nominal exchange rate [$:£]) : $ price of US good. Also, real exchange rate is constant where exchange rate follows purchasing power parity theory

281	**Effective Exchange Rate**	The exchange rate of a country's currency measured against a weighted average of the currencies of its major trading partners

Additional information:
This gives a general picture of whether the nominal exchange rate movements of, say, £ Sterling against all other currencies have made exports relatively more expensive for foreigners; the weights used reflect the % trade with each country; trend in effective exchange rate is given in index number form

282	**Purchasing Power Parity** (PPP)	The nominal exchange rate which ensures home produced goods cost the same if bought abroad

Additional information:
i.e. Big Mac costing £3 in UK and $6 in US would imply PPP exchange rate of £1 = $2 since £3 buys a Big Mac in UK and US (after being converted into $); PPP exchange rates are arguably the most appropriate for making international comparisons of living standards

Section D:	**Growth and Development**

283	**Standard of Living**	A measure of the material well-being of a person

Additional information:
Linked to the flow of goods and services (including leisure) a person can afford to consume; no generally accepted measure (weighted average of GDP, wealth and leisure per capita)

284	**Quality of Life**	A measure of the overall well-being of a person

Additional information:
An attempt to broaden standard of living to include 'non-material' aspects like political rights, educational and cultural opportunities

285	**Shadow Economy**	Payments for production which go unreported to the tax authorities

Additional information:
Also known as the black economy; where employers pay workers in cash to evade tax (illegally); the larger this sector, the more national income statistics will underestimate living standards

286	**Development**	Broad notion of progress in social and economic conditions within a society covering improved material standards of living, self esteem and expanded opportunities for all individuals

Additional information:
Normative concept; measured by Human Development Index (see also Todaro's objectives); used to classify countries: least/less/more (economically) developed countries (LEDC v MEDC) or developing v developed

| 287 | **Less Economically Developed Countries** (LEDC) | Term referring to those countries with relatively low per capita income |

Additional information:
Less value-laden term for a poor country than 'less developed' or 'developing'

| 288 | **Newly Industrialised Countries** (NICs) | Countries which have rapidly industrialised since 1950 |

Additional information:
The original group of NICs were the East Asian 'tiger' economies: Hong Kong, S. Korea, Singapore, Taiwan; since then several other countries could also be included e.g. China and Mexico

---

| 289 | **Human Development Index** (HDI) | A measure of the relative socio-economic progress within a nation as a weighted (per capita) average of real income, education (literacy, years of schooling) and life expectancy |

Additional information:
HDI uses scores which lie between 0 (the minimum level in any country) and 1 (the maximum); it is a broader measure of development than GDP per capita; in 2007, Iceland ranked top (0.968) when 10th on GDP per head, Niger was lowest (0.281)

| 290 | **Index of Sustainable Economic Welfare** (ISEW) | A broader alternative to GDP as a measure of economic growth in which net contributions to personal welfare are accounted for |

Additional information:
Differs from GDP in that e.g. home production is added but defence spending is subtracted and environmental degradation is accounted for; Friends of the Earth have estimated that Germany's per capita ISEW fell sharply between 1980-86 despite growth in GDP per capita!

| 291 | **Human Poverty Index** (HPI) | A measure of the proportion of national population suffering absolute poverty (defined by access to material necessities like safe water, literacy and life expectancy) |

Additional information:
HPI shows how well development is spread throughout a society; Egypt's HPI was higher than China's despite similar HDI (see 289) indicating greater inequality in Egypt

---

| 292 | **Infrastructure** | The capital making up society's transport and communications networks, its supply of basic amenities and key public services |

Additional information:
e.g. road, rail and telephone network, supply network for electricity, water and gas, schools and hospitals; sometimes called 'social overhead capital'; its absence is a major impediment for a region's economic development

293 **Subsistence**	Where farming families produce food for their own consumption
	Additional information:
	This is widely practised in poorer, largely agricultural societies; it forms part of the unrecorded or informal sector so official per capita income/GDP understates standards of living

294 **Cash Crop**	Agricultural crop which is produced for the export market
	Additional information:
	Often the legacy of a colonial past; the danger is that export earnings from cash crops go largely to the elite who run the industry, leaving the workers on small incomes; farmland can be tied up with the cash crop leaving locals to face food shortage

295 **Brain Drain**	The emigration of highly skilled workers (domestically trained) who are able to earn far higher salaries abroad
	Additional information:
	A major constraint on growth in poorer economies since their skills are lost to the domestic economy, however social ties limiting time abroad and money sent home offset this

296 **Debt Crisis**	Constraint on economic growth facing LEDCs due to growing proportion of their national income needed to service the debt to richer economies
	Additional information:
	Measured by: debt service ratio = debt service (i.e. interest) payments/export earnings per year; if high, interest repayments can only be met with greater borrowing, which is unsustainable; in 1997 10 countries had debt higher than their GNP!; since then rich creditor nations have tried to tie debt relief to poverty alleviation

297 **Capital Flight**	The withdrawal of funds from a country due to poor economic conditions, hastened by a speculative fear of currency devaluation
	Additional information:
	This actually pushes the domestic exchange rate down further, which usually requires government steps to support the exchange rate, like raising interest rates, to guard against inflation

298 **Rural-Urban Migration**	Relocation of people from villages to cities
	Additional information:
	Necessary to boost economic growth because urban industrial work has greater scope for productivity gains than agriculture; but scale and speed can be excessive which pressurises city infrastructure

299	**Demographic Transition**	Model where population grows according to four phases as a country develops economically

Additional information:
1. High birth and death rates (deaths per population, per year) – traditional subsistence society (steady population); 2. Death rate falls – industrialisation (population grows); 3. Birth rate falls (population growth slows); 4. Low birth and death rates – post-industrial society (steady population)

300	**Rostow's Stages of Growth**	Model where a country's economy grows according to five phases

Additional information:
1. Traditional rural; 2. Preconditions for take-off (entrepreneurs appear, improvement in transport etc.); 3. Take-off (industrialisation: investment rates double); 4. Drive to maturity; 5. Mass consumption; model (from 1960) criticised as overgeneralised

301	**Industrialisation**	Early stage of economic development where proportion of national output from manufacturing grows rapidly as agriculture's share declines

Additional information:
Associated with rural-urban migration and rising average incomes because manufacturing offers work of higher productivity (more capital per worker) and has faster growing market

302	**Deindustrialisation**	Later stage of economic development where proportion of national output from manufacturing declines steadily as the share from the service sector rises

Additional information:
For UK, this process has been especially marked since 1989: share of GDP taken by manufacturing has fallen from about 23% to 15% (2008), although in absolute terms manufacturing output has been rising very slowly (up 5% over this period); by contrast Germany's manufacturing share has hardly fallen over 1997-2008 (still around 23% GDP)

303	**Harrod-Domar Growth Model**	Model asserting national economic growth depends on increases in its savings rate and decreases in its capital-output ratio

Additional information:
Savings rate = savings/income, raising this necessarily raises investment rates which produce growth; capital/output ratio will be lower when capital is more productive (for example where technological advance occurs)

304	**Terms of Trade**	Ratio of an index of a country's export prices to an index of its import prices

Additional information:
The terms of trade is said to 'improve' when it rises because a given quantity of exports will earn enough to buy more imports than before; less developed countries relying on primary products face terms of trade 'deterioration' over time as such necessity commodities are often income inelastic e.g. tea (Sri Lanka)

| 305 | **Prebisch-Singer Hypothesis** | Hypothesis that countries which specialise in primary products will suffer falling terms of trade over time |

Additional information:
Often a problem facing less developed countries; demand for these exports are price and income inelastic, hence primary product prices plummet when technological advance drives up supply or invents a synthetic substitute, and price of manufactured goods rises relatively faster when world income rises

---

| 306 | **Foreign Direct Investment** (FDI) | Investment in physical capital abroad by multinational companies |

Additional information:
e.g. the purchase of a foreign company or the setting up of a production plant abroad; less developed countries receive much of this because labour costs are lower; it has a beneficial impact on employment and often involves technology transfer which has spin-off benefits for other local firms

---

| 307 | **Import Substitution** | Strategy used by LEDC governments to replace imports of manufactured goods with domestic production |

Additional information:
Popular in 1960s in countries like India; typically involved tariffs to keep imports uncompetitive; growth rates paled against the export-orientated industrialisation strategy alternative used by the NICs; failed perhaps because resources are not allowed to move to their most profitable use when the state intervenes

---

| 308 | **OECD** | Organisation for Economic Cooperation and Development |

Additional information:
An organisation to promote economic growth amongst over twenty of the richest economies e.g. G8, Hungary, Mexico, Turkey, Australia and New Zealand; also aims to help LEDCs

---

| 309 | **UNCTAD** | United Nations Conference on Trade and Development |

Additional information:
Branch of the U.N. which aims to promote world trade and help LEDCs in this area

---

| 310 | **UNDP** | United Nations Development Programme |

Additional information:
Branch of the U.N. that finances and carries out development projects in LEDCs

311	**International Monetary Fund** (IMF)	Institution designed to stabilise the world's financial system, stepping in when exchange rates move dramatically and where countries experience severe Balance of Payments problems

Additional information:
IMF lends to governments whose exchange rates are falling fast or whose Balance of Payments current account is in growing deficit. Recipient nations must accept conditions which enforce tighter monetary and fiscal policy and supply side measures like privatisation ('Stabilisation Programme'), which target low inflation; such neo-classical 'shock therapy' can create short term unemployment and cause reduced growth, which worsen the LEDC's plight

312	**Stabilisation Programme**	Conditions attached to loans from the IMF designed to strengthen macroeconomic performance

Additional information:
Typically includes monetary and fiscal contraction and supply side measures like trade liberalisation (removing tariffs etc.); designed to reduce inflation and support the exchange rate in the long term; but it often hits poorest hard and exposes domestic firms to greater risk of bankruptcy

313	**World Bank** (IBRD)	International financial institution which provides funds for development projects

Additional information:
International Bank for Reconstruction and Development (official title); lending is usually at market rates of interest (hence is not 'aid') but International Development Association (branch of the World Bank) lends interest free with long repayment periods to the poorest countries; voting power is proportional to contributions (i.e. favours richer countries)

314	**Structural Adjustment Programme**	Conditions attached to loans from the World Bank designed to strengthen microeconomic performance by encouraging market friendly institutions

Additional information:
Overlaps with typical stabilisation (macro) measures, especially concerning supply side reform

315	**Non Government Organisations** (NGOs)	Private sector organisations (like charities) involved in providing financial and technical assistance to LEDCs

Additional information:
Complements the aid offered by rich economy governments, but without serving overtly political aims. Thus it is argued that NGOs provide more reliable, better targeted aid

316	**Intermediate Technology**	Technology appropriate to the needs of a LEDC

Additional information:
Therefore it enables improvements in labour productivity without being so capital intensive that jobs are lost; it is less sophisticated than that used in richer economies e.g. spades rather than combined harvesters (for which lack of spare parts may prove a further difficulty)

317	**Aid**	Transfer of resources to LEDCs on concessional terms which aim to promote economic development

Additional information:
Can be grants, soft loans, technical assistance or transfers of commodities (e.g. famine-relieving food); bilateral if from one country or multilateral if through international agency like EU or World Bank)

318	**Tied Aid**	Aid provided by a rich economy on condition that the recipient uses the funds to buy products from the donor country

Additional information:
Form of bilateral aid, which may be less useful than unconditional aid since recipients cannot freely buy the best help available

319	**Soft Loan**	Loan which is provided to a LEDC at concessionary rates

Additional information:
e.g. with interest repayment rates at least 25% lower than market rates, or with very long repayment periods

	Section E:	**Basic Macro Economic Concepts**

320	**Economic (or business) Cycle**	The tendency for market economies to grow in a cyclical pattern typically over a period of 5 to 10 years

Additional information:
Such cycles have been well documented for over 150 years in the economically advanced economies: there is a period of 'boom' in which real national output grows relatively fast (say 5% +, for 2-3 years), but which brings about high inflation and a 'bust' in which real growth goes negative during a recession and unemployment soars; causal factors: accelerator and multiplier; since 1945 most governments have tried to dampen down the cycle using demand management (e.g. reducing tax to stave off 'bust')

321	**Output Gap**	Actual GDP minus sustainable GDP

Additional information:
Over the course of an economic cycle (boom to boom: usually 5-10 years) the average annual growth of real GDP can be estimated (for UK recently this has been 2-3%): in boom years real GDP will exceed this trend creating a positive output gap, implying GDP growth driven by high AD creating inflationary pressure; negative output gap arises in recession implying AD can rise without causing inflation

322	**Progressive Tax**	A tax which takes a higher proportion of income as income rises

Additional information:
Essential for tackling inequity ('fairer'); e.g. UK income tax, since poorest pay very little (tax free allowance + lower marginal rates of tax until get richer); shift away from direct taxation since 1979 in UK since thought to act as disincentive to work and politically unpopular compared to 'stealth' (indirect) taxes; in UK, overall effect of direct and indirect taxation is broadly proportional (since progressive direct taxation offset by regressive indirect tax), with each quintile paying about 35% of disposable income in tax

323	**Regressive Tax**	A tax which takes a lower proportion of income as income rises

Additional information:
e.g. VAT (despite zero rated goods) or tobacco duty since poor spend more of their income than the rich; shift to indirect taxation since 1979 in UK (advantage: better for incentives to work; disadvantages: regressive + inflationary)

324	**Marginal Rate of Tax** (MRT)	The proportion of an additional pound of income which goes in tax

Additional information:
= change in tax paid/change in money income; e.g. top rate income tax has MRT of 40% in UK; cuts in MRT should stimulate AD (via C) and AS (higher incentive to work)

325	**Automatic Stabiliser**	A feature of the government's public finance which helps keep aggregate demand stable in the face of 'booms' and 'busts' (the business cycle) without a deliberate attempt by government to adjust AD

Additional information:
e.g. benefit payments to unemployed (in recession these automatically rise, which raises AD; vice versa for booms, which protects against threat of inflation); also progressive income tax (in boom these receipts rise as people move into higher tax brackets, hence reducing AD at the right time and vice versa for recessions)

326	**Discretionary Fiscal Policy**	Alterations to fiscal policy (government spending and taxation) deliberately made by government to modify Aggregate Demand in pursuit of its macroeconomic policy aims (low inflation, high growth etc)

Additional information:
Also known as 'fine tuning'; in contrast some fiscal factors work automatically e.g. entering recession leads to lower tax withdrawals and higher benefit payments (thereby stimulating AD when it is needed most) via these 'automatic stabilisers'

| 327 | **Transfer Payments** | Spending by government on cash benefits to certain groups which is not in exchange for productive output |

Additional information:
Examples: pensions, job seekers allowance, child benefit etc.; this element of government spending is usually designed to improve equity (distribution of income from rich to poor); is not included as part of the G item in the aggregate demand equation (: AD = C + I + G + X – M)

| 328 | **New Deal** | New Labour's policy to combat long term unemployment: after a period of assisted job search, an unemployed person is guaranteed some form of paid work (voluntary work or subsidised employment) or training |

Additional information:
Launched in April 1998 for the 18-24 age group, it now covers many other unemployed; the rationale is that periods of unemployment diminish human capital because people lose self esteem and skills through lack of practice; benefit is withdrawn if person refuses to cooperate; New Deal is a supply side policy to make labour market more flexible

| 329 | **Public Sector Net Cash Requirement** (PSNCR) | Government spending minus revenue (per year) |

Additional information:
Also known as budget deficit; result of reflationary fiscal policy designed to raise AD (and employment etc); needs financing by either borrowing from banks (inflationary) or selling bonds to general public (raises interest rates – offsetting some of the boost to AD: 'crowding out'); national debt is the outstanding debt of a national government at a point in time: large if fed by series of budget deficits; Public Sector Debt Repayment is budget surplus

| 330 | **Demographic Timebomb** | The negative effects of the ageing of the populations in the industrialised world |

Additional information:
Causes: 1. falling birth rates; 2. increased life expectancy; 3. early retirement. Effects: rising dependency ratio (= population of non working age/ population of working age) leading to increased pension spending by government. Possible solutions: raise taxes on workers, reduce pension rates, raise retirement age, move from taxpayer funded to private or (Stock market) funded pensions

| 331 | **Deflationary Policy** | Government policies to reduce aggregate demand |

Additional information:
3 measures: i. increase interest rates (monetary policy), ii. cut government spending (fiscal policy), iii. raise taxes (fiscal policy); aims to reduce inflation (or trade deficit/boost £ exchange rate) but trade off is lower growth and higher unemployment (unless AS curve is vertical)

332 Fiscal Drag

The effect of inflation (or even real earnings growth) which increases the tax burden in a progressive income tax system without government raising tax rates because people move into higher tax brackets

Additional information:
This would enable government to raise the relative size of the public sector by stealth; its effect is to reduce AD (more T, less C) unless government spends the extra tax revenue; each Budget, the Chancellor must raise tax thresholds by the rate of inflation (or real earnings growth) to remove fiscal drag

333 Fiscal Boost

The effect of inflation to reduce the real burden of unit taxes over time unless government indexes unit taxes or moves them in line with inflation

Additional information:
In UK this affects the duties on tobacco, alcohol and petrol e.g. if inflation is 10% and petrol duty kept at 50p per litre (when full price is £1), tax burden falls from 50/100 to 50/110; effect is to raise AD (less T, more C in real terms)

334 Laffer Curve

The relationship between average rate of income tax and tax revenue: at low tax rates, raising tax rates will increase revenue but after a point revenue falls as workers lose the incentive to work

Additional information:
Part of neo-Classical theory popular in early 1980s which inspired Reagan (US) and Thatcher (UK) to cut income tax rates as a way of encouraging work and enterprise AND raising more revenue for vital state spending (e.g. defence and policing)

335 National Debt

Outstanding debt of a national government at a point in time

Additional information:
Often mistaken for the country's residents' debt to foreigners, whereas the national debt is usually owed by government to its own general public, who have bought government bonds to finance an annual budget deficit (PSNCR); EMU members must keep national debt below 60% of GDP; high national debt implies high interest payments (leaving less tax revenue for public services)

336 Golden Rule

UK Government must only borrow for investment projects: all current spending (non-durable items, like wages) must be paid for from current year tax receipts

Additional information:
Adopted by Chancellor Gordon Brown in 1998 to ensure 'fiscal prudence' and put downward pressure on public spending. Increases in public spending must be accompanied by tax rises unless benefiting future generations, which justifies borrowing so raising the repayment burden on those generations

337	**Sustainable Investment Rule**	UK Government must ensure national (i.e. public sector) debt never exceeds 40% of national income

Additional information:
Adopted by Chancellor Gordon Brown in 1998 to reassure its creditors (buyers of government bonds) that it will be able to repay its debts ('fiscal prudence'); whilst government can always raise funds by taxation, if national debt/national income rises too high the debt interest proportion of public spending may get out of control; Euro membership requires (softer) 60% debt ratio

Section G:	**Advanced Macroeconomic Theory**

338	**Quantity Theory**	Classical theory explaining inflation as the result of excessive monetary growth

Additional information:
MV = PT; money stock (M) x velocity of circulation of a unit of currency per year (V) = amount spent; average price level (P) x number of transactions (T) = value of output bought; if T rises at long term trend growth (2%?) and V is constant, any monetary growth in excess of 2% will be inflationary; problems: V may vary, M is hard to measure (broad or narrow money?), inflation could be caused by cost push factors exogenous to the model leading to rises in M

339	**Inflation Target**	Policy that monetary conditions will be adjusted if forecasted inflation moves away from a declared target

Additional information:
UK policy since 1992; until Bank of England's independence in 1997, Government decided whether to adjust the base rate; since then, Government sets the target (currently 1-3% CPI) and the Monetary Policy Committee decides interest rate monthly (it is raised to prevent inflation overshooting target or cut to prevent an undershoot)

340	**Loanable Funds Theory**	Theory explaining the determination of interest rates (the price of money) via the demand and supply of loanable funds (money)

Additional information:
Demand for loanable funds is inversely related to interest rate (consumers and businessmen borrow more when repayment rates are lower) whereas supply is positively related (savers will want to save more when bank savings rate are higher); equilibrium exists at the single interest rate at which demand matches supply; curve shifts explain rate changes e.g. during a consumer boom, demand for loanable funds shifts right which leads to rate rises (Bank of England merely respond to market conditions)

341	**Marginal Propensity to Consume** (m.p.c.)	The proportion of an increase in income which is spent on domestically produced consumer goods and services
		Additional information: A higher m.p.c. means any injection (spending) will raise incomes by a higher multiple: Multiplier = $1/(1 - \text{m.p.c.})$
342	**Marginal Propensity to Withdraw** (m.p.w.)	The proportion of an increase in income which is not spent on domestically produced consumer goods and services
		Additional information: A higher m.p.w. means any injection (spending) will raise incomes by a smaller multiple: Multiplier = $1/\text{m.p.w.}$; m.p.w. = sum of marginal propensities to save, tax and spend on imports
343	**Accelerator**	Principle of investment theory whereby investment spending by firms responds to *change* in demand (or GDP)
		Additional information: Hence, a slowing in demand growth produces a fall in I, but I rises before demand bottoms out; interaction between accelerator and multiplier can exaggerate the boom-bust economic cycle
344	**Phillips Curve**	Inverse relationship between rate of wage inflation and unemployment in the macro economy
		Additional information: Empirically based; the short run relationship reflects shifts in AD as economy slides up/down (upward sloping) SRAS curve; In long run, Classical Economists believe the economy will settle at a natural rate of unemployment (NAIRU) consistent with those voluntarily unemployed: attempts to reflate and drive unemployment below this natural rate will simply raise inflation and only reduce unemployment so long as the 'money illusion' lasts
345	**Non Accelerating Inflation Rate of Unemployment** (NAIRU)	The 'natural' unemployment rate at which demand for labour matches supply of labour in the macro economy (leaving only voluntary unemployment)
		Additional information: At NAIRU there is no pressure on wages or prices up or down; part of Classical economic theory implying government should target low inflation (monetary expansion to match real GDP growth) and not try to manipulate AD to fight unemployment; supply side policies can reduce NAIRU

346	**Monetarism**	The belief that monetary policy is the main way for government to effectively run the macro economy

Additional information:
The underlying belief is that rises in aggregate demand from expansionary monetary or fiscal policy will only ever boost real output in the short run at best, the labour market adjusting to the NAIRU in the long run once people fully anticipate inflation; also that inflation control requires monetary contraction via the Quantity Theory (338)

347	**Keynesianism**	The belief that the macro economy can reach an equilibrium even with much unemployment and that then expansionary fiscal policy is a more effective solution than monetary policy

Additional information:
Hence the Keynesian AS curve is upward sloping but not vertical; implies that wages are 'sticky' downwards in a recession, causing demand deficient unemployment; fiscal stimulus (like increased spending on public works) raises AD via the multiplier whereas interest rate cuts may just be saved instead, especially if there is deflation

348	**Deflation**	Situation of persistent negative inflation

Additional information:
A climate of falling average prices means consumption is deferred in expectation of lower prices, which reduces real growth via a downward multiplier; interest rate cuts may become ineffective once nominal interest rate reaches zero (with falling prices this still implies a positive and rising real interest rate, which deters recovery of AD)

349	**Rational Expectations Theory**	The belief that all economic agents are able to forecast the macro economy based on an understanding of macroeconomic theory and act accordingly

Additional information:
Hence a policy of boosting AD to encourage real growth below the NAIRU will be instantly recognised as inflationary and the voluntarily unemployed will not be tempted into work by a rise in nominal wages which they mistakenly perceive as a rise in real wages

Index of Economic Terms